STANDAF

Capital Investment
Decision-Making

Capital Investment
Decision-Making

DERYL NORTHCOTT
University of Manchester

The Chartered Institute of
Management Accountants

INTERNATIONAL THOMSON BUSINESS PRESS
I ⓉP An International Thomson Publishing Company

London • Bonn • Boston • Johannesburg • Madrid • Melbourne • Mexico City • New York • Paris
Singapore • Tokyo • Toronto • Albany, NY • Belmont, CA • Cincinnati, OH • Detroit, MI

Capital Investment

Copyright © 1998 International Thomson Business Press

I(T)P® A division of International Thomson Publishing Inc.
The ITP logo is a trademark under licence

British Library Cataloguing-in-Publication Data
A catalogue record for this book is available from the British Library

First published 1992 by Academic Press Limited.
Reprinted 1995 by Dryden Press and 1998 by International Thomson Business Press.

Printed in the UK by TJ International, Padstow, Cornwall

ISBN 1-86152-458-7

International Thomson Business Press
Berkshire House
168–173 High Holborn
London WC1V 7AA
UK

http://www.itbp.com

Series Editor's Preface

David Otley
KPMG Peat Marwick Professor of Accounting
Lancaster University

A major problem for the management accounting teacher has been the selection of a suitable text for advanced courses. Although a number of very good texts exist, they typically do not include some topics that individual teachers wish to teach. On the other hand, they do include a considerable amount of material on topics that are unnecessary for a particular course. Students often feel that they have a poor deal in purchasing large and expensive texts that do not cover the whole of their course, yet include large amounts of extraneous material.

This series is an attempt to resolve this problem. It will consist of a set of slim volumes, each of which deals with a single topic in depth. A coherent course of study may therefore be built up by selecting just those topics which an individual course requires, so that the student has a tailor-made text for the precise course that is being taken. The texts are aimed primarily at final year undergraduate courses in accounting and finance, although many will be suitable for MBA and other postgraduate programmes. A typical final year advanced management accounting option course could be built around four or five texts, as each has been designed to incorporate material that would be taught over a period of a few weeks. Alternatively, the texts can be used to supplement a larger and more general textbook.

Each text is a free-standing treatment of a specific topic by an authoritative author. They can be used quite independently of each other, although it is assumed that an introductory or intermediate-level management accounting course has been previously taken. However, considerable care has been taken in the choice and specification of topics, to ensure that the texts mesh together without unnecessary overlap. It is therefore hoped that the series will provide a valuable resource for management accounting teachers, enabling them to design courses that meet precise needs whilst still being able to recommend required texts at an affordable price.

Preface

It is an unfortunate requirement that to make money, an organization usually has to spend money – the trick is always in spending it wisely. Making decisions about what is and isn't worth spending money on is never easy, especially where the expenditure is large and the returns are risky, as is generally the case with capital investment.

This book considers the task of capital investment decision-making. The behavioural aspects of this activity are examined, along with the quantitative tools available to assist in evaluating capital investment options. Capital investment is viewed here as an integral part of the strategic and operational functioning of an organization. Having read this book, the reader should be able to competently apply financial analysis methods to CI proposals, while at the same time having a broader appreciation of the implications of the investment decision for the organization and the people within it.

Initially, traditional notions of CI decisions are explored. A generally accepted model of the CI "process" is proposed and the reader is introduced to the analytic techniques which have developed from this view of CI. The information required as input to these analyses is considered, and some of the practical difficulties of getting this information are examined. Techniques which have been developed in response to these difficulties are presented and discussed.

Having established a "traditional" approach to CI decision-making, the reader is then presented with a review of the literature which documents CI practice as it occurs in many organizations. Here the reader is confronted with the apparent gap between theory and practice which is reflected in this literature. There remains much of practice that is little understood and some of the difficult issues in CI, as perceived by practitioners, are identified and discussed.

In exploring this apparent theory–practice gap this book goes on to consider an alternative, but complementary, view of the nature of CI. Behavioural and organizational aspects of this decision-making activity are considered and the reader is encouraged to consider some of the problematic qualitative issues of CI. As an exercise in applying this broad perspective, a case study of a CI decision is presented. The reader's task is to "look into" the organization presented in the case and gain some appreciation of the complexity of investment decisions as they occur in practice.

The book concludes by identifying current areas of advancement in CI decision-making theory and practice, and by challenging the reader to consider the role of the management accountant as an information provider within organizations where such major investment decisions must be made. It is the hope of the author that the reader will learn not only to be technically competent in the quantitative examination of investment options, but also to be aware of the organizational context of these decisions. If such a balance can be achieved, then the reader may go on to make positive contributions to these decisions within organizations, taking a step towards closing the gap between theory and practice.

Acknowledgements

There are many people who have provided help and encouragement during the writing of this book. Thanks are due to my colleagues at the University of Waikato for their support and ideas. In particular this book has benefited from the critical thinking and comments of Alan Lowe, the superior computer graphics skills of Nikki Sayer (for her great work in putting together the Appendix) and the spreadsheet expertise of Ed Vos. Also, the contributions of Stewart Lawrence, Mike Pratt and others in creating an environment in which it is a pleasure to work, have been particularly valuable.

Finally, my special thanks go to David Otley for his support and assistance in bringing this book to life, and to my husband Grant for keeping me sane!

Contents

Glossary

Accounting rate of return (AROR): The average annual accounting profit generated by an asset, divided by the investment the asset represents or the average investment over the asset's life.

Annuity: An investment which produces a regular, constant stream of cashflows for a limited number of periods.

Annuity factor: A multiplicative factor used to find the present (or future) value of the stream of cashflows arising from an annuity. An annuity factor depends on the required rate of return and the number of periods for which the annuity continues.

AROR: See *accounting rate of return.*

Asset beta: A measure of the variability of an asset's returns relative to overall market movements. Asset beta is peculiar to the *type* of asset only, and independent of the way in which the asset is financed.

Beta: A measure of the variability of returns from a financial instrument relative to overall market movements.

Capital asset: Any asset or investment whose financial effects extend beyond the short term.

Capital asset pricing model (CAPM): A theoretical model which suggests that the expected returns on all risky assets are a function of their covariance with the market portfolio.

CI: See *capital investment.*

Capital budgeting: The activity of making long-term decisions about selecting and financing capital assets.

Capital investment: The activity of making, communicating and implementing decisions about investment in long-term, risky capital assets.

Capital investment proposal: A suggestion for expenditure on a capital investment project, to be considered by capital investment decision makers. Often capital investment proposals are formal documents requiring specified information to be presented in a standard format.

Capital rationing: A shortage of funds which forces an organization to choose between competing investment projects. Capital rationing can be either externally imposed ("hard" rationing) or internally imposed ("soft" rationing).

CAPM: See *capital asset pricing model.*

Compound: To find the future value of an amount invested. Any interest arising from the initial investment is assumed to be reinvested to form part of the principal in a following period. Compounding is the opposite of *discounting.*

Cost of capital: The cost of obtaining funds to finance the capital expenditure of an organization, or the return required to compensate an investor for the cost of obtaining funds to finance an investment.

Covariance: A statistical measure of the extent to which variables move together.

DCF: See *discounted cashflow*.

Depreciation: A non-cash expense which recognizes the reduction in the value of a capital asset over its estimated useful life.

Differential cashflow: A cashflow which eventuates, or is altered, as a direct result of the investment decision under consideration.

Discount: To find the present value of a future cashflow (the opposite of *compound*).

Discounted cashflow (DCF): A cashflow (usually occurring in the future) which has been discounted, i.e. expressed in present value monetary terms.

Discounted payback period (DPP): An approach to investment analysis in which the cashflows from an investment are discounted at some required rate of return, and the time taken for these discounted cashflows to recoup the *initial outlay* is calculated.

Discount rate: (See also *required rate of return*). The rate of return at which future cashflows are discounted in order to express those cashflows in equivalent present value monetary terms.

Dividend payout: The amount of cash paid to shareholders, usually expressed as a percentage of the *earnings per share*.

DPP: See *discounted payback period*.

Earnings per share (EPS): The amount of profit earned by an organization, divided by the number of equity shares issued.

EPS: See *earnings per share*.

Equity beta: A measure of the variability of returns to the equity owners of an asset, relative to movements in the overall market. Equity beta is influenced by the *asset beta*, and the way in which the asset has been financed.

Game theory: An approach to selecting between uncertain options (e.g. potential investments). Game theory often seeks to minimize the loss from a bad decision, rather than to seek means of ascertaining the optimal choice.

Incremental cashflow: See *differential cashflow*.

Inflation index: A factor by which cashflows can be multiplied in order to take account of the effects of inflation in increasing the future amount of that cashflow.

Initial outlay: The amount required to be spent on the purchase and installation of a capital asset so that an asset (or investment) can become operational. Cashflows pertaining to the initial outlay are normally said to occur in "time period zero", i.e. immediately at the start of the investment's life.

Internal rate of return (IRR): The discount rate at which the cashflows from a capital asset produce a zero *net present value*. The internal rate of return thus expresses the return earned by that capital asset.

IRR: See *internal rate of return*.

Linear programming: A mathematical (usually computer-driven) decision model concerned with how best to allocate scarce resources in order to maximize or minimize a given objective.

LP: See *linear programming*.

Minimax: The selection of the best of those worst-possible outcomes which may eventuate from an uncertain undertaking, using *game theory*.

Minimax regret: The selection of the option, from within a group of uncertain options, which minimizes the opportunity cost (or "regret") of making a bad choice, using *game theory*.

Monte Carlo simulation: See *simulation*.

Net present value (NPV): The value, expressed in present-day monetary terms, of the net cashflows resulting from a capital asset. The net present value of an asset depends on the *discount rate* used to convert future cashflows to their present-day value, as well as the size and timing of the asset's cashflows.

Nominal required rate of return: A *required rate of return* which takes into account a factor for the effects of inflation, and which should be used to discount nominal (i.e. inflated) future cashflows.

NPV: See *net present value*.

Operations research (OR): The application of scientific (often mathematical) methodologies to assisting problem-solving in an organizational system, e.g. capital investment decision-making.

Opportunity cost of capital: The return required to compensate an investor for the lost opportunity to employ funds elsewhere and earn a known rate of return. Opportunity cost of capital is normally at least equal to the *cost of capital*, but may exceed the cost of obtaining funds if lucrative alternative investment options exist.

OR: See *operations research*.

Payback period: The time taken for the cashflows (un-discounted) from a capital investment to recoup the required *initial outlay*.

PE ratio: See *price-to-earnings ratio*.

PI: See *profitability index*.

Portfolio: A combined holding of more than one risky asset by an investor.

Post audit: (Otherwise known as post completion audit, post investment appraisal, performance audit and ex post audit). A post audit is an appraisal of the performance of a capital investment project after that project has been implemented and is demonstrating its realizable operating results.

PP: See *payback period*.

Price-to-earnings ratio (PE ratio): The ratio of the current market price of an equity share to the organization's current annual *earnings per share*.

Profitability index (PI): The ratio of the future value of cashflows occurring from a capital investment to its required *initial outlay*.

Real required rate of return: A *required rate of return* which excludes any factor for inflationary effects, which should be used to discount real (i.e. not inflated) future cashflows.

Return on investment (ROI): The returns (usually measured by accounting profit) generated by an investment or group of investments, divided by the amount of investment (either initial or average) required to achieve those returns.

Required rate of return (RRR): The rate of return which must be achieved on an investment to compensate the investor for the use of funds (see also *discount rate*).

Risk: The variability of expected returns from an investment. Risk relates to known variables, to which probabilistic outcomes can be attached, and is normally measured by the statistical measures of standard deviation or covariance.

Risk averse: Preferring less risk. Rational investors are assumed to be risk averse since they will normally require a greater return to compensate them for higher risk, and/or will accept a lower return for a lesser risk investment.

Risk-free rate: The rate of return which will compensate an investor for the use of funds in a risk-free investment project.

Risk premium: The premium which is added to the *risk-free rate* to compensate an investor for the use of funds in a risky investment. The size of the risk premium is related to the degree of riskiness of the investment.

ROI: See *return on investment*.

RRR: See *required rate of return*.

Securities market line (SML): A theoretical construction of the *capital asset pricing model* which plots the linear relationship between differing assets' riskiness and their corresponding expected *required rates of return*.

Sensitivity analysis: Analysis of the effect on an investment project's financial results of changes to key variables (such as the *discount rate*, expected cashflows and the life of the investment).

Simulation: An approach to establishing the riskiness of a project, where multiple risk elements exist. Simulation requires that probabilities be assigned to the foreseeable range of each of these risky elements. A probability distribution of overall outcomes is achieved by repeatedly calculating overall outcomes, randomly selecting each variable value from the pre-designated probability distributions. (Also known as "Monte Carlo simulation".)

SML: See *securities market line*.

Time value of money: The recognition that the value of money changes across time, e.g. £1 received at some time in the future has less value than £1 received today. In order to convert money amounts in differing time periods to a common unit of measure we often *discount* the future amounts to express them in present value equivalents.

Uncertainty: The possibility that an actual amount will deviate from an expected amount. No probability can be assigned to the possible outcomes of an uncertain variable, and uncertainty encompasses the behaviour, and existence, of those variables which were completely unanticipated.

WACC: See *weighted average cost of capital*.

WDA: See *writing down allowance*.

Weighted average cost of capital (WACC): A composite of the individual costs of each source of financing (e.g. ordinary equity, preference shares and debt). The weighted average cost of capital is a function of the cost of each of these financing sources, and their relative weightings in the overall financing structure.

Working capital: The excess of current assets over current liabilities, i.e. the net amount of investment in assets which have an expected life of normally less than twelve months.

Writing down allowance (WDA): A tax deductible allowance set by taxation authorities, which acts as a *depreciation* allowance to recognize the reduction in the value of a capital asset over its useful life. The writing down allowance spreads an asset's initial purchase cost over its life for income reporting and taxation purposes.

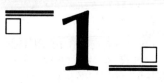

What is Capital Investment?

CAPITAL INVESTMENT DEFINED

Many people, in many organizations, spend a great deal of their time making decisions about capital investment. This book will explore techniques which assist this decision-making activity, considering the organizational environment within which capital investment decisions are made. But as a starting point, it is useful to establish a definition of just what capital investment is.

Capital investment (CI) can be seen as a sub-set of capital budgeting. Capital budgeting refers to both the selection of long-term investments, and planning for their financing. Capital investment is concerned with the former, although it should be recognized that the financing decision is integrally related to the investment decision. Both impact upon each other. However, deciding which projects should be undertaken as capital investments is sufficiently problematic to warrant consideration on its own, and is the focus of this book.

Many definitions of CI have been proposed. In the main, these definitions have several common elements, which can be summarized as follows:

1. The investment generally involves a substantial financial outlay.

1

2. The returns from the investment occur over a number of years in the future.
3. There is generally some element of risk and uncertainty in predicting what these future returns will be.
4. The types of investment typically considered to be CIs include the purchase or expansion of equipment or production facilities, or other expenditures which directly impact upon the organization's ability to meet its strategic and operating objectives.

However, there are some important features of CI and its associated decision-making requirements which have usually been omitted from standard definitions. The ways in which CI decisions relate to, and impact upon, other aspects of organizational activity should also be considered as an integral part of the CI activity. Similarly, implications which CI can have for the behaviour and evaluation of organizational employees is also a significant concern.

Taking these broader issues into account, a more appropriate definition of CI can be proposed:

Capital investment requires the making, communication and acceptance of decisions about investment in long-term, risky capital assets. These decisions take place within social organizational contexts and impact upon the strategic and operating position of the organization, and also upon those people who constitute the organization.

Therefore, we would expect CI decisions to take into account the strategic and behavioural implications of the proposed investment, as well as some rigorous examination of its financial effects.

The types of expenditure which constitute capital investments can vary between different organizations. For example, a potter who runs her own business might be considering purchasing a new replacement kiln for £3,000. The types of questions which might be relevant to such a purchase include:

- how much will the new kiln cost to run, compared with the old kiln?
- by what amount will it increase output capacity?
- will the new kiln be more reliable?
- will it help to improve the quality of the pottery?

Spending £3,000 might be a considerable expenditure for a small business, and making a good decision about this potential capital investment could be a key factor in the future success of the business.

On a larger scale, a multinational oil company might be considering whether or not to construct a new refinery, at a cost of hundreds of millions of pounds. The basic questions which are relevant to the decision could well be similar to those in the small business example: how much will it cost to buy and to run, and how will it change output, reliability and quality? Yet clearly, an oil refinery is a quite different concern from buying a potter's kiln!

The common ground between these two examples can be found in our definition of CI. The investment decision will affect the people in the organization and the future success of the business, and involves an amount of expenditure which is significant in the scheme of the organization's financial position. Therefore, in considering what CI is about and how CI decisions are made, there are many issues which apply to all types of organization. No matter what asset is being purchased, or what project is being considered, there is much to be gained from using good CI decision-making practice.

WHO IS INVOLVED IN MAKING CI DECISIONS?

There is no one answer to this question. Evidence from surveys of practice suggest some variation in the people who may participate in CI decisions, even though much of the prescriptive literature suggests that these decisions are the domain of the accountant. As with most decisions, the information input is often richer the more people are consulted, and it is common to see any or all of the following personnel contributing:

- accountants/financial managers
- operational managers
- line staff (who often work with the capital assets)
- production personnel
- engineers
- specialist capital investment officers/committees
- general managers and boards of directors (who are often responsible for the final decision to commit to large items of expenditure).

It is rarely the case that CI decisions are made behind the closed doors of the accountant's office. Although accountants have an obvious role in providing financial analysis and advice, specialist operational or technical expertise is often required to assess the relative merits of potential investments in long-term assets. Similarly, the size of expenditure may mean that a CI decision must gain the approval of people occupying senior positions in the organization. Therefore, as we might expect, CI decisions can be complex, requiring a "meeting of minds" of people with different expertise and perceptions of the investment. Information-gathering, communication, debate (even lobbying) and the achievement of consensus (whether shared or imposed), are all major issues in CI decision-making.

THE SIGNIFICANCE OF CAPITAL INVESTMENT

Decisions made about CI are significant at two levels: for the future operability of the organization making the investment, and for the economy of a nation as a whole. Capital investment involves the directing of significant resources towards particular areas of economic activity. So collectively, CI decisions made by individual organizations impact upon the future economic position of a nation.

At an organizational level, decisions about the commitment of resources to long-term capital assets have implications for many aspects of operations. Capital investment often concerns the purchase or modification of plant and machinery used in manufacturing, so the cost, range, quality, innovation and leadership of products are all affected by capital investment decisions. The adoption of new technology, both in manufacturing and information management, may be subject to scrutiny as a capital investment. Therefore, the very information systems available to organizational decision-makers must normally be justifiable as appropriate capital expenditures. Similarly, the future competitive position of firms which compete in technologically advancing industries is often shaped by decisions about technology investment.

It is clear that, for many organizations, money spent on long-term assets constitutes a significant proportion of expenditure and has an important impact upon future operability. The same is true, in aggregate, for a nation's economy. Miller (1988) has noted the way in which some of the CI appraisal techniques, outlined later in Chapter 3, were embraced by economists and academics alike in the 1960s as a bright, new hope for securing economic prosperity. Some authors of the time were raising concerns with economic growth. For example, Merrett and Sykes (1963, p. xii) noted that, in Britain, "concern over our inadequate rate of growth has reached significant proportions". They suggested that the poor British economic growth was due less to "an inadequate amount of investment" than to "the quality of the investment which [was] at fault". Miller quotes Alfred (1964), who was Chief Economist with Courtaulds Ltd at the time when he proclaimed his interest in a newly emerging CI analysis method:

> it leads to a marked change in the emphasis of investment policy which I believe can significantly affect the rate of growth of individual companies and of the economy as a whole.

So, improved CI decision-making has been, and continues to be viewed not only as an important issue for individual organizations, but as a potential panacea for economic growth. Academics, economists and practitioners alike have concerned themselves with understanding the attributes of "successful" CI decisions, and encouraging decision-makers to use better techniques to assure quality investment.

HOW DOES CAPITAL INVESTMENT RELATE TO OTHER ORGANIZATIONAL ACTIVITIES?

As with any other aspect of organizational activity, CI cannot be adequately considered in isolation. Capital investment shapes, and is shaped by, many other functions and decisions which constitute the organization. Also, CI decisions must be responsive to an organization's external operating environment.

Figure 1.1 characterizes the interactive relationships between CI decisions and other facets of organizational activity, recognizing that these relationships occur within a dynamic organizational environment which is itself impinged upon by an exogenous operating environment. The relationship between CI decision-making and financing decisions has already been noted as one which incorporates both the selection and financing of investment projects. Research and development, production and information management all rely to varying extents upon the commitment of funds to long-term investments, so can be seen to clearly relate to CI decisions. The financial reporting function must grapple with ways of representing the value of CIs whose uncertain returns are to occur in the future and do not meet traditional financial accounting standards of objectivity.

Marketing has perhaps a less obvious relationship with capital investment. Yet, market research, advertising and the setting up

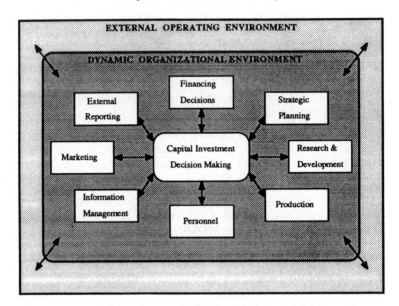

Figure 1.1 Capital investment decisions and the organization

of distribution networks (for example) all involve substantial financial outlay in return for uncertain future benefits. Product design and quality control overlap with the production planning function, and are affected by decisions to commit capital to production facilities. Marketing can therefore be seen as a capital investment issue.

Strategic planning, as a long-term, forward-looking activity, has clear associations with capital investment. Capital investment should be undertaken in close association with strategic planning to ensure a match between an organization's long-term objectives and the direction of resources towards achieving those objectives. In fact, CI decision-making is often seen as an integral part of the strategic planning activity.

Later the relationship between CI decision-making and issues of organizational personnel will be examined more closely. Behavioural implications of CI decisions have rarely been considered, and there are significant potential conflicts between CI decision-making techniques and personnel performance measures which need to be reflected in approaches to capital investment. Organizational personnel have an important place in our picture of how CI decision-making relates to, and interacts with, facets of organizational activity.

SUMMARY

In this chapter we have considered a definition of capital investment which brings together traditional notions of quantitative financial analysis and a broader dimension of organizational and behavioural implications of CI decision-making. It has been noted that capital investment is a significant decision-making activity which not only affects the future operability of an individual organization, but also has wider implications for a nation's economy.

The remainder of this book will identify and discuss the differences between the "traditional" approach to CI which focuses upon quantitative financial analysis, and the orientation suggested in this chapter where CI is seen as an integral part of an organization's environment. Next we consider this "traditional" understanding of CI. The reader should attempt to identify aspects of this understanding which appear inconsistent with the "organizational approach" reflected in the definition of CI proposed in this book.

Suggestions for further reading

Bower, J.L. (1970). *Managing the Resource Allocation Process: A Study of Corporate Planning and Investment*, Richard D. Irwin Inc., Homewood, Illinois.

Brealey, R.A. and Myers, S.C. (1991). *Principles of Corporate Finance* (4th edn), McGraw-Hill Inc., New York.

Horngren, C.T. and Foster, G. (1991). *Cost Accounting: A Managerial Emphasis* (7th edn), Prentice-Hall Inc., Englewood Cliffs, N.J.

Pike, R. and Dobbins, R. (1986). *Investment Decisions and Financial Strategy*, Philip Allan Publishers Ltd., Oxford.

Turton, R. (1991). *Behaviour in a Business Context*, Chapman & Hall, London.

Wilson, D.C. and Rosenfeld, R.H. (1990). *Managing Organisations, Texts, Readings and Cases*, McGraw-Hill, London.

Problems

1. What do you think might be the implications for practice of embracing a "traditional" definition of, and approach to, capital investment decision-making?
2. Consider how a marketing manager might assess the viability of expenditure on a significant promotional campaign which is expected to produce future increases in sales. What quantitative, and qualitative, factors might be taken into account?

3. Find three other definitions of capital investment (sometimes also referred to as capital expenditure, or capital budgeting). Compare and contrast the elements of these definitions.
4. What difficulties might you expect to be encountered in incorporating the views of accountants, line managers and engineers when considering a potential capital investment? What measures would you consider appropriate in attempting to reconcile these possible differences?
5. "The problem with some people is that they forget we're here to make money! In the end, all of our investments must show a good financial return, and so crunching the numbers correctly is all that really matters when we make these decisions." Discuss this view.

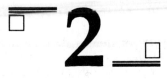

The Capital Investment "Process"

INTRODUCTION

Capital investment has traditionally been understood as an ordered process. The word "process" connotes a mechanistic image of CI, where information flows into some "black box" where it is digested and turned into a recommendation for action, which is then implemented as output from the process. This book will later suggest that such a characterization of CI decision-making may not be appropriate, but first it is important to reflect on this approach as the way in which CI is commonly understood.

This chapter will present and deconstruct a typical model of CI decision-making which has several identifiable stages:

- project identification
- project definition and screening
- analysis and acceptance
- implementation
- monitoring and post audit.

Each stage of this process will be defined and described, and an overview of the main issues of these stages is presented. The CI model presented in this chapter will later form a basis for considering the financial analysis tools which have been developed to assist this decision process.

THE CAPITAL INVESTMENT MODEL

As with many aspects of human decision-making, people have attempted to model the way in which CI decisions are made. There have been many variations of such models, but they tend to share similar characteristics. Figure 2.1 shows the main components of a typical model of the CI process. In Figure 2.1 the CI process is depicted as occurring within the domain of the organizational environment, although the nature of interaction between CI and other facets of the organization is unclear. However, it is usually recognized that CI decision-making takes place within an organizational context.

In a similar vein, strategic planning "floats around" as part of the context of CI decisions, but with uncertain impacts. Generally, it is noted that potential CI projects must be compatible with an organization's strategic plan, as they help to shape the future direction of the organization. Yet, just how strategic planning and CI decision-making fit together is rarely captured in diagrammatic representations of CI activity.

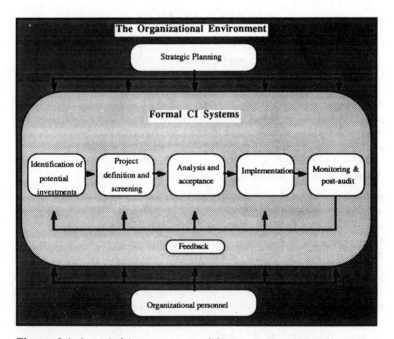

Figure 2.1 A capital investment model

Also, it is recognized that appropriately skilled personnel must be available to oversee and implement selected projects, as well as to come up with CI project ideas and make the investment decisions. However, the roles that different people (in different positions) may play in the CI process are not easily reflected in such models. So, the "people component" often lies outside the representation of the formal CI system.

It may also be noted from Figure 2.1 that there is generally assumed to be some formal CI system in place in an organization, within which this decision process operates. That is, guidelines (perhaps procedural manuals and standardized documentation) provide a framework for the decision process, and information systems exist to ensure that decision-makers have access to the necessary decision input. Rarely do we see informal communication channels or procedures featured in such models of the CI process.

What *does* seem to be commonly accepted is that the CI decision-making "process" is reflected by a feedback, cybernetic-type model. Let us consider the elements of this typical model.[1]

IDENTIFICATION OF POTENTIAL INVESTMENTS

Recognition of a potential investment is the starting point of the CI process. King (1975, p. 73) called this stage the "triggering" phase of CI, and noted that, although much capital investment theory assumes that potential CI projects exist and simply need to be discovered, "in practice each opportunity for investment must be identified and exploited". Pike and Dobbins (1986, p. 3) accredit this stage of the CI process with much importance in securing successful outcomes, stating that "the prosperity of a business depends more on its ability to *create* profitable investment opportunities than on its ability to *appraise* them".

Often ideas for capital investment come from people who work in technical positions. For instance, a plant manager is perhaps in the best position to identify ways in which expanded capacity or updated machinery can increase the output or efficiency of a production process. Survey research conducted by Petty, Scott and Bird (1975, p. 162) revealed that, while lower organizational levels collectively account for more investment proposals than do higher levels, proposals for new product lines were more likely

---

[1] Later the reader will be introduced to evidence of what actually happens in practice. Bear in mind that this empirical evidence may not support the model proposed here.

to come from higher organizational levels. This seems consistent with the expectation that higher-level personnel would have a "strategic" view of the organization's direction, and would focus rather more on innovation in the market place and the competitive environment.

However, the knowledge and initiative required to come up with ideas for good CI projects are difficult to prescribe in any textbook. Perhaps the most important rule is to create an environment in which organizational members feel free to present and develop ideas. One possible mechanism is to develop a two-step approach to encouraging investment ideas, by allowing undeveloped ideas to be proposed, with the option of committing funds to further exploration and refinement of those which seem promising, and screening out those which do not. Later we will consider how performance appraisal systems can play a part in encouraging innovation and the active search for CI ideas.

PROJECT DEFINITION AND SCREENING

The generation of CI ideas leaves an organization with just that – ideas. Turning these ideas into operational formulations of spending requirements, implementation practicalities and quantifiable future benefits is the difficult activity known as "project definition".

Obtaining the information required for full project definition is often costly. For example, the project initiator may require engineering specifications, quotes from suppliers, and marketing information before an investment idea can be given any workable shape and form. For this reason, like idea generation, project definition may occur in two stages. First, enough detail is derived to allow preliminary screening of the project to ensure that it warrants further investigation. Once this initial "go-ahead" has been given, further project definition is required before any detailed financial analysis can be undertaken.

It is often during this definition stage that the project initiator develops personal commitment to a CI idea. As the initiator gathers information, he or she must continually reassess the project, and often must convince colleagues of its feasibility. These colleagues may also begin to support the proposal, and so commitment to it grows. The more commitment a project achieves, the more likely it is to be ultimately approved.

Although it is usually expected that all possible variations of a potential CI will be presented impartially for appraisal, project

Initiators may in the definition stage have consciously, or unconsciously, eliminated some of the options. Since project definition directly precedes the analysis and acceptance stage, the screening which takes place here is influential in deciding which projects will finally be accepted for investment. Those projects which never go on to be formally analysed are unlikely to ever see the light of day. Even those projects which do proceed to formal analysis may be affected by early screening. Information filtered out at this stage can direct the project's development more than the detailed financial analysis which may follow. For this reason, project definition must be treated as an important part of the CI process, with as many people as possible contributing to and refining these early ideas.

Preliminary screening of CI proposals which may occur at this stage is often based on qualitative evaluation of a proposal, addressing fundamental questions of project viability. For example, a CI idea which is clearly unprofitable, physically impractical, or not in keeping with the organization's overall strategy is likely to be eliminated here before further cost is incurred in project definition and financial evaluation. It may also be the case that "politically unacceptable" projects go no further than a preliminary screening.

After a proposal for CI has been sufficiently well defined and has met preliminary requirements of feasibility and desirability, it then moves on to more rigorous assessment in the next stage of the CI process.

ANALYSIS AND ACCEPTANCE

The quantitative financial analysis of proposals has been the focus of much of the prescriptive CI literature. The techniques which have been developed to assist this analysis are outlined later. There are several basic approaches to financially analysing CI projects, of varying degrees of technical sophistication. The reader will see that these techniques require that all aspects of a CI project can be quantified (usually monetarily) and evaluated, using criteria which serve to maximize shareholder wealth (the assumed goal of the organizational decision-maker). The CI decision-making model suggests that it is at *this* stage that a decision is made whether to invest in a proposed CI, based on the outcome of the financial evaluation.

Steps involved in analysis and acceptance – an overview

The analysis and acceptance stage may be further broken down into several steps which are generally identified in models of the CI decision process. These steps are as follows:

1. Completing and submitting "standard format" financial information as a formal CI proposal. Many organizations have standard procedures for presenting CI application information. An example of standard application documentation is presented in the Appendix, p. 186.
2. Classifying the proposed CI by "type". Classification of projects by type usually separates projects into those which require more or less rigorous financial appraisal, and those which must achieve a greater or lesser rate of return in order to be deemed acceptable.
3. Performing appropriate financial analyses on the information provided in support of the CI application. It is here that the financial implications of the project are assessed.
4. Comparing the outcome of these analyses to predetermined acceptance criteria. A. CI project must meet or exceed established financial criteria to be acceptable.
5. Considering the proposed project within the CI budget for the current (and future) operating periods. Where funds available for investment are limited, the CI budget should be considered before an investment decision is made.
6. The decision to approve, or reject the proposal. It is here that the final decision is taken to commit the organization to CI expenditure.
7. If the proposal is approved, establishing requirements for the monitoring and implementation of the CI project development and expenditure.

In different organizations each of these steps may be emphasized to a greater or lesser extent. However, it is generally accepted that all these steps are essential components of the analysis and acceptance stage of the CI decision process. Let us now consider each of these steps in greater detail.

The CI proposal

The information required for the analysis and acceptance stage of the CI process is more detailed than that required for initial screening purposes, and must be justified by the project initiator.

Many organizations develop standard forms for completion by anyone applying for CI expenditure approval (again, see the Appendix, p. 186 for an example). Usually, the project initiator is required to consider a range of project options, identifying those which appear preferable after preliminary evaluation. It is also useful at this stage to identify "key variables" in the CI proposal, so that these factors can form the focus of sensitivity analysis, and be emphasized in ongoing monitoring should the project be implemented.

Often organizations have defined time periods during which CI proposals are accepted for consideration. These periods may correspond to annual budget-setting, where the financial controllers seek an early indication of what CI expenditures can be expected in the forthcoming budgeting period. Alternatively, an organization may accept CI proposals on a regular basis throughout the year (e.g. monthly), allowing greater scope for investment in unanticipated opportunities. However, it may be the case that projects previously foreshadowed for the annual CI budget receive preferential funding over those which were not.

Project classification

As noted earlier, capital investment proposals are often classified by type, so that different acceptance criteria can be applied to differing categories of investments. These classifications vary between individual organizations, but a typical grouping might be as follows.[2]

1. Replacement of existing assets.
2. Expansion of existing operations.
3. Strategic expenditure to develop new types of production, technologies or product lines, perhaps repositioning the organization in the market place, or responding to some change in the operating environment.
4. Non-financially motivated expenditures, e.g. safety, environmental or legislatively required expenditures (often exercises in cost minimization).

Alternative (or supplementary) classifications may relate to how essential an expenditure is perceived as being (see Rosenblatt and Jucker, 1979) or the size of the expenditure (see Gitman and Forrester, 1977). Clearly, the classification of CI types is judge-

---

[2] Runyon (1983) identified this type of classification in his study of CI decision-making in small US firms.

mental. This has important implications when we consider that the financial analysis undertaken on a CI proposal could be dictated by the category to which the project is initially allotted.

Financial analysis

Once a CI project has been classified, most organizations will have an established requirement for the financial analysis of projects within each category. Since most organizations are in the business of making money (or at least, of not *losing* money), financial analysis is an important part of the CI decision-making process.

Sometimes further information will be sought at this stage, or CI proposals may be sent back to the initiator for reformulation. The people undertaking the financial analysis must be satisfied that they have sufficient information for the analysis they are to perform. Of course, some types of projects (e.g. safety or regulatory projects) have less stringent information requirements, as the financial analysis outcome is less likely to affect the ultimate decision.

The formal, financial analysis of a CI proposal can take several forms, and may be conducted by differing groups of people. Some organizations rely on a project initiator (usually in liaison with an accountant) to prepare projections of expected expenditures and financial benefits. Others have specialized staff who act as CI controllers, or form CI committees whose task it is to check the costs and benefits of a CI, and to assess and compare all CI proposals.

The types of financial analyses commonly employed in assessing CI proposals are considered in Chapter 3. Broadly speaking, they fall into two groups: non-discounted cash flow methods (considered to be "unsophisticated"), and discounted cash flow methods (considered "sophisticated"). Whichever methods are used, the emphasis of this phase of the CI process is on assessing those aspects of the proposals which can be quantified in monetary terms. While an important factor in arriving at a decision, these financial analyses rarely constitute the entire basis for a CI decision, in practice. Indeed, it is not usually desirable that financial analyses be emphasized to the exclusion of other considerations.

Acceptance criteria

In order that financial analyses should have some purpose, the decision-makers must be able to relate the analysis results to some predetermined "bench-marks" or acceptance criteria. These criteria will vary, depending upon the type of financial analysis undertaken, and the class of investments into which a CI proposal has been initially categorized.

For example, a straightforward asset replacement project may be required to achieve a 14 per cent return, while an experimental venture into a new market may be considered more risky and may be required to return 20 per cent.[3] Acceptance criteria for financial returns are usually less stringent for a less risky project.

Also, organizations may adopt different financial criteria depending on the time horizon for which they consider CI returns. Although CI decisions are normally considered to be long-term, many firms require short-term performance criteria to be met also. For example, where short-term liquidity is a concern, an assessment of the timing of a project's early cashflows might be considered together with its overall long-term performance.

Acceptance criteria are usually established taking into account not only the "type" and risk of project, but also the cost to the organization of funds, and the historical levels of financial importance. A more detailed consideration of how these factors may impact upon CI acceptance criteria is presented later.

Considering the CI budget

Also during the analysis and acceptance stage, we see the interrelationship between the investment and financing decisions. Often the financing decision incorporates budget-setting, limiting the amount of funds which the organization makes available for CI. Budget limits may be imposed externally, perhaps by scarcity of financing, high financing costs which the organization perceives as prohibitive, or by debt covenants which restrict the amount of external financing an organization may seek. Alternatively, budget constraints may be imposed internally, often where managerial resources are limited. The imposition of internal budget restrictions is known as "soft capital rationing", whereas external limits constitute "hard" capital rationing.

Whether or not a proposed CI project has been foreshadowed in the organizational budget may influence the way in which it is assessed in this analysis phase. For example, the budget-setting process may require submission of outlines of forthcoming CI

---

[3] The meaning of "required rate of return" will be explored in later chapters.

projects. This allows the budget to take into account likely expenditure on essential or financially rewarding projects. These outlines may require some preliminary financial justification for submitted projects, lessening the need for financial analysis at a later stage.

Projects which emerge *during* a budgeting period can be disadvantaged, as they may have less early commitment from senior personnel, and they will not have funds "set aside" in the budget. Where funds are limited, such emergent projects may be subjected to rigorous financial analysis to justify their usurping of a project which has been previously foreshadowed in the CI budget.

The decision – accept or reject?

"Go" and "no-go" decisions on CI projects may be made at different hierarchical levels of an organization, depending on the type of investment, its perceived riskiness and the amount of expenditure required. For example, an organization may allow a divisional manager to have CI expenditure authority up to £30,000, a regional manager up to £100,000, and a group general manager up to £250,000, requiring approval from the board of directors for any greater amount.

Once the accept-or-reject decision has been made, the organization is committed to the CI project. Along with this commitment comes responsibility. The decision-maker must now accept that the project's success or failure will inevitably reflect on his or her ability to make good decisions.

Systems for monitoring and implementation

Once CI decisions have been made, the organization must plan for the implementation and monitoring of approved CI projects. This usually requires the assignation of responsibility for each CI to a "project manager". This is often someone technically skilled in the area on which the CI will impact, who may consult with finance and accounting staff. Alternatively, some organizations may take a team approach to implementation, calling on people from all areas of the organization to contribute to the setting up of the new project.

It is useful at this stage to design any required subsequent post audit of a project, taking into account the key variables upon which the review should focus and the responsibility of personnel for providing project information. If post audit requirements are considered from the outset, it is much easier to obtain relevant information on the performance of a CI project.

Analysis and acceptance: summary

Once a CI project has gone through this analysis and acceptance phase, the commitment to a project is made. Information has been gathered, financial justification established, the budget consulted and the final go-ahead given by the appropriate people. Once the mechanisms are in place, the next phase of the CI process can take place – implementation.

PROJECT IMPLEMENTATION

It is the task of the project manager to oversee the physical construction or installation of capital assets, and to undertake such ongoing monitoring as is required by management.

The physical aspects of project implementation usually require a team approach, where people with expertise in a variety of relevant areas can contribute to the successful development of a CI project. Examples of specific tasks which must be performed at this stage include reviewing engineering specifications, obtaining quotes for equipment or construction requirements, ensuring that suppliers can make appropriate commitments to the needs and timing of the project and arranging for any necessary retraining of employees.

Monitoring can be by way of physical measures (e.g. the number of units of production resulting from a new manufacturing installation), financial measures (e.g. how much has been spent), or a combination of both. The implementation of a CI project also requires the setting up of effective information systems which can provide feedback on progress, results and key variables identified as being crucial to the performance of the project.

It should be possible to check whether spending is incurred as per the initial project outline, and whether "benchmark" performance variables or timing criteria are met. Deviations in these factors should signal a need for review, thus allowing ongoing monitoring systems to identify problems while there is still time to correct them. The effective use of ongoing project monitoring goes some way towards reducing the need for the next stage of the CI process – post audit.

POST AUDIT

Post audit is often discussed interchangeably with ongoing project monitoring. However, since it occurs *after* the project has run a significant part of its life, post audit has less potential to correct problems in current projects than it has to improve future CI decision-making. Post audit provides follow-up to a CI project. The success of a CI project is assessed (ideally using the same criteria as were employed in the analysis and acceptance phase of the CI process), and reported to interested parties.

For example, a CI project entailing the installation of a new production line might be reviewed after it has been in operation for an entire production cycle. That way, implementation costs and ongoing performance for the new production line can be observed and compared with initial estimates submitted in the CI proposal. Often, especially with large CIs, there is a time-lag between project approval and the asset becoming operative. This can make post audit less timely, but there is often a trade-off between timeliness and the reliability of the post audit information.

A post audit review should focus on those aspects of an investment which have been identified as particularly sensitive or critical to the success of the project, rather than necessarily being a comprehensive review of all aspects of the investment. Post audits are time-consuming and costly, and so careful consideration should be given to the cost–benefit trade-off ensuing from the post audit results. Many organizations make limited selections of CIs to be post audited, concentrating on those which required the greatest expenditure, or which we perceived as most risky or strategically important.

The timing of post audits can vary, although they are usually conducted after a CI project has reached a stage of its life where its relative success can be ascertained. That is, the project must usually be up-and-running, and have produced results over a sufficiently long period to create confidence that these results reflect the project's continued operations. As a result, post audit is generally concerned more with feedback into the overall CI process, than with useful, corrective feedback on a particular project.

There are a number of potential advantages of conducting post audits. Horngren and Foster (1987, p. 696) identify what they call

a threefold desirability of follow-up:

1. to see that spending and specifications conform to the plan as approved

2. to increase the likelihood that capital-spending requests are sharply conceived and honestly estimated, and
3. to improve estimation on future capital budgeting projects.

Horngren and Foster go on to say that "the very existence of follow-up helps in this regard", and note that "this function is vital to a successful capital-budgeting program". So, the main benefit of post audit may be the impact which its very existence has on the behaviour of project initiators. People who know they will be held accountable for results will usually take more care in their initial estimations of the costs and benefits of a CI. Also, the feedback provided by post audit can provide useful information for improving future decisions, by identifying problems in defining and quantifying CI projects.

Collecting the information for use in a post audit review is often problematic. Since the CI project initiator may have a personal interest in representing the success of a project, post audit should usually be undertaken by an independent person or group, such as an internal audit department or a designated CI projects officer. However, this person or group must somehow obtain information relating to the project. If the project initiator has influence over the information presented to the post audit personnel, there is potential for biased reporting of CI results. These problems may be addressed by carefully considering the performance appraisal of project initiators/overseers as part of the post audit outcome.

SUMMARY

This chapter has identified a typical model of the CI decision-making process and has outlined the main elements of each stage of the process, as they are commonly understood in the prescriptive CI literature. Each of these stages is important within the CI model, but in practice may be emphasized to a greater or lesser extent by any organization.

The tools and techniques for financially evaluating CI proposals which will be developed in the next chapter have emerged from such a characterization of CI decision-making as an ordered, structured process. The reader should keep this CI model in mind, and note that the quantitative CI decision support tools relate almost entirely to the "analysis and acceptance" stage of the CI process.

Suggestions for further reading

Chartered Institute of Management Accountants (1984). *Capital Expenditure Control*, CIMA, London.

Dillon, R. and Caldwell, J. (1981). "A system for post auditing capital projects", *Managerial Planning*, Jan–Feb, pp. 18–22, 30.

Gadella, J. (1986). "Post auditing the capital investment decision", *Management Accounting (UK)*, November, pp. 36–7.

Neale, B. and Holmes, D. (1988). "Post completion audits: The costs and benefits", *Management Accounting (UK)*, March, pp. 27–30.

Pike, R.H. and Wolfe, M.B. (1988). *Capital Budgeting for the 1990s: A Review of Capital Investment Trends in Larger Companies*, The Chartered Institute of Management Accountants (Occasional Paper Series), London.

Problems

1. Discuss the differences between the kinds of information which would be used for the preliminary screening of a CI project and that required for formal financial analysis.

2. Explain the "feedback loop" in the CI process. How might post audit findings impact on the other stages of the CI process?

3. Outline the potential benefits of conducting CI post audits. What factors might influence the decision whether to conduct a post audit on a particular project?

4. If you were the CEO of a large organization with many production divisions, how might you encourage people within the organization to identify and explore ideas for CIs?

5. Aharoni (1966) has written that:

   > in order to collect information, it is necessary to communicate with people, to make certain decisions, and often to give tacit promises. In this process commitments are accumulated until a situation is created which leads inevitably to investment.

   Discuss this suggestion with reference to the CI decision-making model proposed in this chapter.

6. Discuss ways in which the CI decision-making "process" might differ between large and small organizations.

3

Financial Analysis Tools for CI Appraisal

INTRODUCTION

We have already seen that the CI "process" has an analysis stage at which information pertaining to a CI proposal is used to produce an answer – "invest, or do not invest". It is here that the decision is made whether to proceed to the next stage of implementation.

In this chapter the components of this analysis process are examined. First, the question of what information is relevant to a CI decision will be explored. Once the relevant information has been identified, there is then a choice of methods which may be used for analysing this information.

The theoretical foundations of the main approaches to CI analysis will be outlined as a starting point. Then, distinctions are drawn between those methods which arise from accounting concepts of financial performance, and those which are based on economic notions of wealth maximization. The relative merits and weaknesses of these methods will be discussed, and it will be demonstrated that the economics–derived analysis techniques have superior theoretical support in facilitating "rational" financial decisions.

After working through this chapter, the reader should have a good technical and practical understanding of the techniques which are widely proposed, and used, to support CI decision-making.

WHAT INFORMATION IS RELEVANT TO A CI DECISION?

The short answer to this question is: anything that *changes* as a result of a CI decision will be relevant to assessing the viability of that investment. That is, the CI decision-maker must identify relationships between the decision made, and the costs and benefits which accrue from it, either immediately or in the future.

Some typical examples of relevant information include:

- the purchase and installation cost of the capital asset
- changes in revenues or costs
- required increases in working capital items (e.g. inventory).

Ascertaining this information is often more difficult than it would first appear. For example, the purchase price of a fixed asset is often the only explicit component of the initial outlay cost. Other less obvious costs might include installation, legal costs, retraining of employees, redundancy payments associated with the discontinuation of present employees, and production set-up costs. Capital investment decision-makers must be careful that they have considered all such effects of implementing a CI project.

A number of irrelevant factors are often incorrectly included in the analysis of proposed CIs. Examples include:

- sunk costs (costs already incurred which cannot now be changed, no matter what decision is made)
- future costs and revenues which would have accrued regardless of the current CI decision
- allocations of fixed costs (where the total cost to the organization will not change, even though the way it is allocated for reporting purposes may)
- financing costs (these are already taken into account in the required rate of return imposed on a CI proposal – more of this later).

Again, asking the simple question: "will these costs or revenues change as a result of the decision made?" is usually enough to reveal their relevance (or irrelevance) to the decision. Of course, it is not always easy in practice to identify all factors relevant to a CI decision. The extent to which future costs and revenues will change may be uncertain, and it can be equally difficult to predict what might happen if the CI is *not* undertaken.

A good example of this dilemma arises with respect to new technology. Failure to invest in new technology can result in a declining base-line of organizational revenues, which is difficult to predict. The question then becomes "how much would we lose if we *don't* invest in this asset?", rather than "how much will we gain if we *do* invest?" Of course, whether designed to improve or protect the status quo, the investment decision will change future results and it is these changes which are relevant to the CI decision.

Example 3.1 considers the determination of information relevant to a CI decision.

EXAMPLE 3.1

Relevant information for CI decision-making

A firm is considering purchasing a new plant. Preliminary research conducted at a cost of £1,000 has indicated that a Beta plant is the best option. The Beta plant would cost £40,000 to purchase, and a loan for this amount would be raised at an interest rate of 16% p.a. Plant installation would require an upgrade of existing premises at a cost of £3,000. The new plant would be allocated a 30% share of the premises' maintenance and depreciation costs of £4,000 per annum and would produce extra revenues of £12,000 p.a. for eight years, but an existing operator would have to spend five hours of his current idle-time overseeing the plant's operations. In addition, work-in-process inventory would have to be increased in value by £2,000. (Tax and depreciation are ignored in this simple example.)

What information is relevant?

The information relevant to the Beta plant purchase decision is:

- the £40,000 purchase price of the asset
- the £3,000 cost of premises upgrading
- additional revenues of £12,000 p.a. received over eight years
- the required £2,000 increase in working capital (inventories).

All other information given here is irrelevant. Past research costs are sunk, and cannot be influenced by the decision. The interest payable on the £40,000 loan will be taken into account in determining the asset's required rate of return, so the interest payments themselves are excluded from any financial analysis. Presumably, the £4,000 p.a. maintenance and depreciation costs on the premises are already being incurred, and so a reallocation of 30 per cent of this cost to the Beta plant will not change the financial position of the firm. Also, the operator is already paid for his current idle-time – the purchase of the plant will simply better employ this operator, it will not incur any additional operator costs.

The first important skill of a good CI decision-maker is the ability to identify relevant information. Next, we shall consider ways in which this information might be analysed to assist the decision-maker in reaching an invest-or-reject conclusion. It is important to precede any discussion of these analysis techniques with a consideration of their inherent theoretical underpinnings and assumptions.

THEORETICAL FOUNDATIONS

There are two main views of financial performance measurement which form the theoretical underpinnings of CI analysis techniques: accounting concepts and economics or finance concepts.

Accounting concepts

Notions of stewardship and accountability, together with the concepts and conventions which operationalize the accounting function, have given financial accounting a particular "view of the world". From an accounting perspective, long-term financial success is measured via profitability, while short-term success places greater emphasis on liquidity.

These two concerns of liquidity and profitability have permeated CI analysis techniques. Liquidity concerns have translated into questions of how quickly a CI can repay its cost, and CI analysis methods have developed which measure the speed at which a project will recoup its own initial outlay. Profitability considerations have led to questions concerning the profit return generated by a CI on the investment it represents. Accounting notions of "profit" and "average investment" have been encapsulated in CI analysis tools which adopt such an accounting view of the world.

These accounting-based methods are popular in practice, especially among CI decision-makers in small and medium-sized firms,[1] and are often referred to as "traditional" methods.

Economics and finance concepts

Economics and finance theory have introduced new notions of financial success. This theoretical perspective is concerned less with liquidity and profitability, and more with the maximization

---

[1] Empirical evidence for the use of these CI analysis techniques is presented in Chapter 6.

of shareholder wealth and the consideration of risk. The maximization of shareholder wealth has become widely accepted as the goal of the profit-motivated firm. Therefore, as CI decision-making is concerned with effective resource allocation, it follows that successful CI projects are those which add to the value of the firm, thus increasing shareholder wealth.

Much as share prices (directly reflecting shareholder wealth) are said to represent the current value of expected future cash returns, the value of CI projects is seen as being the excess of their future returns over their current and future costs. Here the time value of money concept enters into CI analysis, as a means of determining the value of future cashflows. (This concept is developed later in this chapter.) Following from this, a CI is deemed acceptable if its expected cash returns exceed its expected cash costs, and so liquidity (the timing of these cashflows) and profitability (the financial reporting of these cashflows) become less important.

Economic theory has also explored the concept of risk. Not all potential CCI projects are created equal; some have greater inherent riskiness than others. It has been proposed that investors adjust their return requirements to account for risk. That is, the greater the perception of investment riskiness, the greater the return required by the investor to compensate for the possibility that variation in returns might eradicate the financial benefits from the CI.

The combination of wealth maximization objectives (focusing on cash rather than profits) and risk considerations has led to the development of CI analysis techniques quite different to the "traditional" accounting-based methods. Let us now consider the range of techniques commonly proposed for CI appraisal, looking at examples of how they are calculated, and the strengths and weaknesses of each method.

ACCOUNTING-BASED TECHNIQUES

Two main analysis techniques have arisen from the traditional accounting view of measuring financial performance. Perhaps the simpler of the two is the Payback Period (PP) technique.

Payback period

Payback period (PP) is concerned with liquidity. It is a short-term orientated method which considers how soon a CI project will pay itself back. The faster a CI project can recoup its initial cost, the better, under the PP analysis approach. Payback period focuses on the cashflows from a CI project, and the speed at which they are received, rather than on any measure of profitability or overall return.

Decision-makers using the PP criterion must decide on an acceptable PP time horizon as a yardstick for the assessment of CI proposals. The greater the liquidity needs of the investor, the shorter may be the acceptable PP time period.[2] Clearly, the selection of a PP "cut-off point" is arbitrary. Example 3.2 provides an illustrative example of how PP may be used.

EXAMPLE 3.2

Calculation of payback period

A firm is considering investing in a new computer system. The cost of purchasing and installing the computer system is £12,000, and it is expected that the system would produce annual administrative savings of £2,000. The computer is expected to have a useful life of eight years, before becoming obsolete and requiring replacement. The firm considers a CI to be acceptable if it pays back within four years. (Tax and depreciation are ignored.)

What is the computer's payback period?
The initial outlay associated with the computer purchase is £12,000, and at an annual return (savings) of £2,000, its payback period would be:

$$PP = \frac{£12,000}{£2,000}$$
$$= 6 \text{ years}$$

Should the firm purchase the computer system?
The answer depends on the PP criterion. Since the firm has established a cut-off point of four years, this asset would not be purchased under a PP decision model.

Of course, CI projects do not always have expected cashflows which are the same each year. In the case of uneven cashflows, a cumulative total of cash inflows must be used to assess a project's PP.

---

[2] Chapter 6 reviews empirical evidence of the PP criteria adopted by firms in practice.

EXAMPLE 3.3

Payback period calculation with uneven cashflows

The expected cost savings associated with the computer system have been revised. It is now expected that savings will improve as staff become more familiar with using the computer system. The pattern of expected cash benefits is now:

Year	Cashflow	Cumulative cashflow
1	£800	£800
2	£800	£1,600
3	£1,500	£3,100
4	£1,500	£4,600
5	£2,500	£7,100
6	£2,500	£9,600
7	£3,200	£12,800
8	£3,200	£16,000

From the cumulative cashflows, we can see that the computer system's payback period has increased. If we assume that cashflows accrue evenly throughout the year, then the CI's payback period is now 6.75 years, even though the total cashflows from the investment (£16,000) remain the same. The project would still not be accepted under the PP criterion.

The PP analysis method has two major deficiencies. First, it ignores any cashflows which occur *after* the project's payback period. In the examples, the benefits accruing from the computer system in years 7 and 8 could have been enormous, yet the PP calculation would have taken no account of them. This deficiency reflects the short-term orientation of the PP technique. Therefore, the use of PP as a decision-making tool penalizes those projects with inherently long lives and promotes those projects which produce rapid returns, even though those returns maybe modest and short-lived.

The second major deficiency of the PP technique is that it ignores the time value of money. A pound received at some time in the future is compared with a pound spent now, as though both have the same value. This will later be shown to be an erroneous comparison. A modified version of the PP analysis method, "discounted payback period" (DPP) has been proposed as a means of overcoming this problem, and will be discussed later in this chapter.

 Payback period is often used in practice. Indeed, there is no harm in performing PP analyses, and they are often useful as a first screening device where an organization is concerned with liquidity. However, PP should not be used as the sole basis for CI decisions, where it can lead to incorrect accept or reject decisions.

Accounting rate of return

The second of the accounting-based CI analysis methods is the accounting rate of return (AROR), sometimes known as the return on capital employed. As its title suggests, this method compares a CI project's "profitability" to the capital employed in the investment. One of the difficulties of this method is that there are many ways of representing "profit" and "capital employed". Alternative profit measures can include or omit financing expenses, depreciation and tax. However, the most common definition of

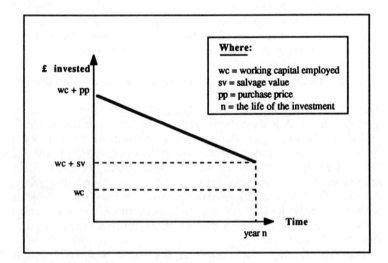

Figure 3.1 Capital employed over the life of an investment

profit used in the AROR analysis is the "earnings before interest and tax" (EBIT) figure, which includes the effects of depreciation.

Two representations of AROR are in common use, using different definitions of capital employed. This can be incorporated as the *initial* capital employed in the investment, or the *average* capital employed over the life of the investment. The initial capital employed usually includes the purchase price and associated set-up costs, together with any increase in working capital required at the outset of the investment. However, at the end of the life of the investment, the capital employed is reduced to the asset's salvage value, plus any remaining working capital component.

The reduction in the amount of capital represented in an investment is illustrated in Figure 3.1. Determining the *average* capital employed is equivalent to finding the area under the curve in Figure 3.1 by adding together the high point (the initial investment) and the low point (the terminal capital employed) and dividing the sum of these by two. Therefore, the AROR formula can be presented in two ways:

$$
\text{AROR} \; = \; \frac{\text{average accounting profit p.a.}}{\text{initial capital employed}} \quad \text{or} \quad \frac{\text{average accounting profit p.a.}}{\text{average capital employed}}
$$

$$
\text{i.e.} \quad \frac{(\Sigma \text{ annual profits}) \div \text{n years}}{\text{Initial outlay}} \quad \text{or} \quad \frac{(\Sigma \text{ annual profits}) \div \text{n years}}{(\text{Initial outlay} + \text{residual value}) \div 2}
$$

Example 3.4 demonstrates the calculation of AROR on both initial and average capital employed.

EXAMPLE 3.4

Calculation of AROR on initial and average capital employed

An asset costs £12,000 to purchase, and has an expected life of five years with a salvage value of £2,000. Additional inventories costing £1,000 are required at the time the asset is commissioned, but can be liquidated for £1,000 at the end of the asset's life. It is estimated that the asset will increase revenues by £5,000 p.a., although it will create a straight-line depreciation expense of £2,000 p.a.

What is the asset's AROR?

The pre-tax profit generated by this asset is (£5,000 − £2,000) = £3,000 p.a. for each of its five years of life. So, using the two different approaches:

Initial capital employed: = (£12,000 + £1,000) = £13,000	Average capital employed: = (Initial capital + terminal capital) ÷ 2 = [£13,000 + (£2,000 + £1,000)] ÷ 2 = (£13,000 + £3,000) ÷ 2 = £8,000
AROR: = £3,000 ÷ £13,000 = 0.23 or 23%	AROR: = £3,000 ÷ £8,000 = 0.375 or 37.5%

The results obtained differ markedly between the two approaches. However, if acceptance criteria are developed consistently with the method to be used, the investment decisions promoted by the two AROR formulations should not differ.

Like the payback period method, AROR is not without substantial flaws. This method uses accounting profit, rather than cashflows, as a measure of return on an investment. It has already been noted that there are many ways of computing accounting profits, making AROR an easily manipulated technique. Inconsistencies in the derivation of profit figures can produce widely differing AROR results, and often these variations are a result of changing accounting policies which may not be immediately obvious to the CI decision-maker.

Also, accounting profits suffer from "distortions" such as depreciation expenses and gains and losses on the sale of fixed assets, which are not actual cashflows and therefore have no real impact on the wealth of the investors.

The second major flaw of the AROR method is shared with the PP method – it does not take account of the time value of money. The return on a CI is deemed to be its average accounting profits, even though these profits occur in different time periods and may change from year to year.

A further problem with AROR occurs when the "average capital employed" method is used. Here, the initial outlay and residual value of an investment are averaged to represent the funds tied up over the life of the investment. The larger the residual value of an investment, the higher becomes the denominator in the AROR formula and the lower is the percentage AROR calculated. Example 3.5 illustrates this point.

EXAMPLE 3.5

The residual value paradox in AROR

Investment A has an initial cost of £20,000 and produces a £5,000 increase in EBIT over each of its five years of life. At the end of five years it has a zero residual value.

Investment B also has an initial cost of £20,000 and produces a £5,000 increase in EBIT over each of its five years of life. However, investment B has a £10,000 residual value.

What are the investments' ARORs?

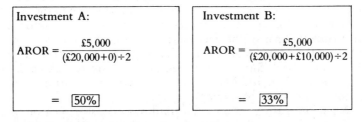

Investment A:

$$AROR = \frac{£5,000}{(£20,000+0) \div 2}$$

$$= \boxed{50\%}$$

Investment B:

$$AROR = \frac{£5,000}{(£20,000+£10,000) \div 2}$$

$$= \boxed{33\%}$$

Using the average capital employed AROR criterion, a zero salvage value investment is preferable to one which retains 50 per cent of its initial value at the end of its life. Yet, clearly B is the better investment as the expected return to the investor at the end of year five is greater.

The residual value paradox illustrated in Example 3.5 is a difficulty of the AROR analysis technique which can lead to incorrect CI decision-making.

It will be shown later that AROR is frequently used in practice as a CI decision support technique. It may be that some CI decision-makers prefer to analyse investments using a method that is consistent with the profit performance measures to which they themselves are subjected as managers. This possibility will be further explored in Chapter 7. Whatever the reason for its use, it is almost certain that reliance on the AROR analysis method is leading to poor CI decision-making in some organizations.

So, it can be seen that the two main "traditional" analysis methods are not ideal. Although both are used in practice, they have serious shortcomings, and can lead to incorrect CI decisions. These techniques have largely fallen from favour in the normative CI literature, and have been replaced with the "sophisticated" techniques whose roots are in economic theory.

ECONOMICS-BASED TECHNIQUES

As a preamble to the "sophisticated" CI analysis techniques, it is important that the reader be familiar with the time value of money concept, and the corresponding mechanics of discounting.

Discounted cashflow analyses and the "time value of money"

Recall that the economic theory approach to measuring an investment's performance is to assess its contribution to the wealth of the investor (or the owners of the firm undertaking the investment). That is, the decision-maker must be able to ascertain whether the value of future benefits from the investment justifies the outlay (and future costs) required to invest. There is an inherent problem in this approach, however, which arises because of the "time value of money".

When comparing inflows and outflows of cash which occur in differing time periods, it is important to recognize that there is a cost associated with forgoing the use of money for a period of time – a pound received today is worth more than a pound received tomorrow.

There are several reasons why the value of money changes with time, which can all be broadly collected under the rubric of "opportunity cost" – that is, if a pound is received now, there exist opportunities for gaining a return on that pound. These opportunities are forgone if the pound is not received until some time in the future. There are several factors which contribute to this effect, namely:

- the forgone opportunity to invest, and earn a return on cash received today
- the erosion of the purchasing power of money over time due to inflation
- natural human preferences for consumption today (which is perceived as certain) over consumption tomorrow (which is less certain).

Therefore, someone who forgoes the use of £1 today so that returns may be received in the future, requires compensation for the reduction in the value of future cashflows. We commonly see this concept in use with interest rates. Interest rates are set at levels which compensate the investor/lender for inflation and risk, as well as providing some return for the loss of use of the money for a period of time. Of course, a range of market interest rates exist at any one time, reflecting differing risk characteristics of investors and lenders. An in-depth discussion of the term structure of interest rates is beyond the scope of this book; it is sufficient for our purposes to acknowledge that any interest rate (or "opportunity cost of money") has three basic components:

1. An inflation component, to ensure that the real purchasing power of money invested today is sustained over time.
2. A "risk-free" return, i.e. a return which pays the investor a "price" for the use of his or her money, assuming that there is no risk associated with the investment. (Government bonds are often used as an indication of the "risk-free return", as governments are perceived as least likely to default on investments.)
3. A "risk premium" which provides additional compensation for any risk associated with the investment. Of course risk premiums vary, depending on the nature of the investment. It is the personal choice of the investor as to whether a high risk–high return or low risk–low return investment profile is adopted.

The concept of the time value of money is simply illustrated by thinking about an interest-earning bank account. If you deposit cash into a bank account today, you can earn interest on it, and receive a larger amount of cash in the future. The rate of interest you earn reflects anticipated inflation,[3] the riskiness of lending your money to the bank, and a "price" which the bank must pay you to persuade you to forgo the immediate use of your money.

EXAMPLE

You deposit £100 for a year, at a 10% interest rate.
At the end of that year, you receive £100 × (1.10) = £110

---

[3] The way in which inflation components are integrated into interest rates/required rates of return is dealt with later in Chapter 4.

So, comparing £100 received today to £100 received in a year's time suggests that the £100 today is worth more, as you have the opportunity to invest it and receive £110 in one year's time. The calculation we perform to find the future value of the investment (i.e. £110) is called compounding, again a familiar concept from the "compound interest" we are accustomed to earning on bank accounts.

The reverse process to compounding is known as discounting. By discounting, we can find the present value of a sum of money received in the future. We can generalize the compounding and discounting formulae as follows:

Compounding:	Where:
$FV = PV \times (1 + r)^n$	FV = future value of a cashflow
Discounting:	PV = present value of a cashflow
$PV = \dfrac{FV}{(1 + r)^n}$	n = the number of years' time in which the cashflow takes place
	r = the required rate of return, or opportunity cost

In our simple example, the present value of the £110 received in one year's time is calculated as:

$$PV = \frac{£110}{(1 + 0.10)^1}$$
$$= £110 \div 1.1$$
$$= £100$$

So, we get back to the original £100 that was invested for a year at a 10 per cent interest rate. Here 10 per cent becomes the opportunity cost (or "discount rate"), i.e. it is the annual rate of return required to compensate the investor for forgoing the immediate use of £100. So, if an opportunity exists to invest money at a 10 per cent annual rate of return, £100 received today has exactly the same value as £110 received in one year's time.

Of course, cashflows can occur many years into the future, and sometimes we come across a regular cashflow, or annuity, associated with a CI. As an alternative to performing lengthy manual calculations, discount and compound tables are available which summarize the multiplication factors appropriate for discounting and compounding at different rates across different time periods.

For example, let us say we want to find the present value of a £5,000 cash inflow which will occur in ten (n) years' time, when we have a RRR of 16 per cent. We can divide the £5,000 by $(1.16)^{10}$, or we can refer to a discount table to obtain a multiplication factor of 0.2267 (see Table 3.1). Either approach will produce the same present value result of £1,133. Similarly, if the £5,000 cash inflow were to occur *every year* for ten years, we could consult a "present value of annuity" discount table to find a multiplication factor of 4.8332 (see Table 3.2). This tells us that the present value of a

Table 3.1 (Excerpt) Present value factors

RRR	6%	8%	10%	12%	14%	16%	18%
n= 5	0.7473	0.6806	0.6209	0.5674	0.5194	0.4761	0.4371
6	0.7050	0.6302	0.5645	0.5066	0.4556	0.4014	0.3704
7	0.6651	0.5835	0.5132	0.4532	0.3996	0.3538	0.3139
8	0.6274	0.5403	0.4665	0.4039	0.3506	0.3050	0.2660
9	0.5919	0.5002	0.4241	0.3606	0.3075	0.2630	0.2255
10	0.5584	0.4632	0.3855	0.3220	0.2697	**0.2267**	0.1911
11	0.5268	0.4289	0.3505	0.2875	0.2366	0.1954	0.1619
12	0.4970	0.3971	0.3186	0.2567	0.2076	0.1685	0.1372

Table 3.2 (Excerpt) Present value of an annuity factors

RRR	6%	8%	10%	12%	14%	16%	18%
n= 5	4.2124	3.9927	3.7908	3.6048	3.4331	3.2743	3.1272
6	4.9173	4.6229	4.3553	4.1114	3.8887	3.6847	3.4976
7	5.5824	5.2064	4.8684	4.5638	4.2883	4.0386	3.8115
8	6.2098	5.7466	5.3349	4.9676	4.6389	4.3436	4.0776
9	6.8017	6.2469	5.7590	5.3282	4.9464	4.6065	4.3030
10	7.3601	6.7101	6.1446	5.6502	5.2161	**4.8332**	4.4941
11	7.8869	7.1390	6.4951	5.9377	5.4527	5.0286	4.6560
12	8.3838	7.5361	6.8137	6.1944	5.6603	5.1971	4.7932

sum received each year for ten years, at a discount rate of 16%, has a present value of 4.8332 times the amount received. We can therefore compute a present value of £24,166. This is a much easier approach than individually discounting the £5,000 cashflows for each of the ten years. Of course, many computer business applications have automatic discounting and compounding functions, allowing present values to be calculated at the press of a button!

The basic concept and mechanics of the time value of money provide a means by which cashflows occurring in different time periods can be correctly compared. The discounting of cashflows to find their present value is the cornerstone of the "sophisticated" CI analysis methods. The first of these methods is known as the "net present value" method.

The net present value method

The net present value (NPV) analysis method compares the *present* value of future cashflows from a CI, with the immediate outlay required. That is, all future cashflows from a CI are discounted back to their present value, and compared with the immediate cost of entering into the investment. Hence the "net" present value is the difference between the present values of the investment's inflows and outflows.

The decision criterion used in conjunction with the NPV method is the same for all investments and all organizations: if the NPV is positive (i.e. greater than zero), then the investment should be accepted. Conversely, if the NPV is negative the investment should be rejected. A positive NPV means that the present value of the CI's inflows exceeds the present value of its costs: therefore an addition to the wealth of the investors is expected. Theoretically, a decision-maker would be indifferent as to whether or not a CI with an NPV of exactly zero would be undertaken. However, intuitively, a zero increase in wealth is usually insufficient reward for the effort of pursuing the investment, and so a zero NPV project would rarely be attractive.

In order to use the NPV analysis method, there are several inputs which must be determined. Broadly the required information includes:

- the CI's required initial outlay
- the relevant future cashflows associated with the CI
- the anticipated life of the CI
- the appropriate discount rate (RRR) to be used.

As noted earlier, determining the initial outlay and future cashflows associated with a CI is rarely straightforward. Similarly, uncertain effects such as wear and tear, obsolescence and changes in the activities of the organization can render asset life estimates incorrect.

Perhaps the most problematic input is the selection of an appropriate discount rate. The discount rate is crucial to the outcome of the NPV analysis, as it determines the relative values of cashflows occurring in different time periods. This issue warrants specific consideration later in this chapter. For the moment, it suffices to note that the discount rate used in NPV analyses should reflect a risk-adjusted RRR.

Let us now consider an example of calculating a CI project's NPV.

EXAMPLE 3.6

The net present value (NPV) calculation

Posa Co. is considering purchasing a delivery vehicle at a cost of £16,000. An employee will be trained to obtain a Heavy Goods Vehicle Licence at a cost of £100. Vehicle running costs are estimated at £3,000 p.a., but Posa Co. will save £7,000 p.a. in contract delivery charges. The vehicle will have a useful life of six years, to be sold for £3,000 at the end of year 6. Posa Co. requires a 12% rate of return on this type of investment (tax and depreciation are ignored).

Detailing the relevant cashflows using a "time-line":

Cashflow	Time 0 (now)	Yr 1	Yr 2	Yr 3	Yr 4	Yr 5	Yr 6
Purchase price	−£16,000						
HGVL	−£100						
running costs		−£3000	−£3000	−£3000	−£3000	−£3000	−£3000
savings on delivery costs		+£7000	+£7000	+£7000	+£7000	+£7000	+£7000
Sale of vehicle							+£3000
Total annual cashflows	−£16,100	+£4000	+£4000	+£4000	+£4000	+£4000	+£7000

All initial outlay costs are said to occur at "time 0" – i.e. now. Note that running costs and savings on delivery contract charges are annuities continuing for the life of the investment. Note also the implicit assumption that cashflows occur at the *end* of each year. For example, the first year's running costs are assumed to occur in one year's time, and will be discounted by one year to obtain their present value. This assumption facilitates simple illustrations, and in practice, where it is difficult to ascertain the exact timing of cashflows, such simplifying assumptions may be used. Finding the vehicle's NPV:

NPV = −£16,100 + (PV of an annuity of £4,000 for six yrs @ 12%) + (PV of a sum of £3,000 received in six years' time, at 12%)

= −£16,100 + (£4,000 × 4.1114) + (£3,000 × 0.5066)

= −£16,100 + £16,446 + £1,520

= +£1,866

The vehicle purchase opportunity has a positive NPV, and should be accepted.

It is useful to think of a "time-line" of cashflows, as presented in Example 3.6. This provides a framework for assimilating the information, and helps in gaining a clear appreciation of the discount factors applicable to each cashflow. The final NPV calculation is simply the sum of the present value of each year's cashflows. It is then a simple matter to base the accept or reject decision on the NPV.

A variation on NPV: the profitability index

The profitability index (PI) measure uses exactly the same discounted cashflow information used in the NPV method. However, instead of finding the *difference* between initial outlay and the present value of future cashflows, the PI finds the *ratio* of these two values. A generalized formula for PI is:

$$PI = \frac{\Sigma \text{ PVs of future cashflows}}{\text{Initial outlay}}$$

For example, if we calculated the PI of the delivery vehicle proposal in Example 3.6, it would be:

$$PI = \frac{£17,966}{£16,100}$$
$$= \underline{1.116}$$

If the PI is equal to 1, future benefits exactly equal outlay costs, and so the firm gains nothing – it is equivalent to a zero NPV. A PI of greater than 1 indicates an acceptable project, while a project with a PI less than 1 should be rejected. The PI approach will always produce the same accept-or-reject decision as the NPV approach, as it is simply a reordering of the same information. However, PI has advantages over NPV where a firm is subject to capital rationing, described in Chapter 4.

Internal rate of return

Internal rate of return (IRR) is the second major CI analysis method to derive from the theoretical perspective of economics. The IRR approach focuses on finding the discount rate at which the NPV of a project would be zero. That is, the IRR is the rate of return earned by the project itself, and equates the present value of future cashflows to the initial outlay. Simple examples illustrate this approach.

EXAMPLE 3.7

IRR calculations

Simple returns
You invest £1,000, and at the end of the year you receive an interest cheque for £120. The IRR of this investment is easily found:

$$IRR = \frac{£120}{£1,000}$$
$$= \underline{12\%}$$

Compound returns
You invest £1000 in Greedcorp. shares. After holding these shares for four years, you sell them and receive £1,810.60. The IRR of this investment can be found by solving the following equation:

FV (£1,810.60) = PV (£1,000) $\times$ (1 + IRR)^4
so: £1,810.60 $\div$ £1,000 = (1 + IRR)^4
so: 1.8106 = (1 + IRR)^4

At this point there are two choices: we can consult a table of compound interest factors to find the four-year rate which has a factor of 1.8106 (16%), or we can solve the equation algebraically:

$$\sqrt[4]{1.8106} = (1 + IRR)$$
so: $(1 + IRR) = 1.16$
so: IRR = $\underline{16\%}$

In practice, finding the IRR of a project often involves complex calculations. Now that computers are so widely available, there are many accounting applications which can automatically compute the IRR of a series of cashflows. However, it aids our understanding of how IRR works to consider a "trial and error" approach to finding the IRR of a CI project. Let us reconsider the delivery vehicle purchase proposal in Example 3.6. We can restate the problem in terms of the IRR. To find the IRR, we set the NPV at zero and solve for the discount rate, that is:

> 0 = −£16,100 + (PV of an annuity of £4,000 for six yrs @ IRR%) + (PV of a sum of £3,000 received in six years' time, at IRR%)

Without the help of a computer, there is no quick way to solve this equation. The simplest manual approach is to repeatedly guess at the IRR until answers are obtained which are close to the required zero. Once we have obtained a discount rate which produces a slightly positive NPV, and a discount rate which produces a slightly negative NPV, then we can interpolate between the two points to find an estimate of the IRR which will give an NPV of zero.[4] This procedure and the interpolation calculations are shown in Example 3.8, using the information from Example 3.6.

EXAMPLE 3.8

Finding a project's IRR by interpolation

The IRR of the vehicle purchase opportunity is the discount rate at which the NPV equals zero, i.e.:

---

[4] It is not essential to have one positive and one negative result. Extrapolation can be used with two positive or two negative results. However, interpolation is a logical approach which is easily illustrated.

0 = −£16,100 + (PV of an annuity of £4,000 for six yrs @ IRR%)
+ (PV of a sum of £3,000 received in six years' time, at
IRR%)

We have already calculated the NPV of this project at 12% as
+ £1,866. Since this result is positive, we must raise the discount
rate to reduce the NPV. Recalculating the NPV using a 16%
discount rate, we get:

NPV = −£16,100 + (PV of an annuity of £4,000 for six yrs @
        16%) + (PV of a sum of £3,000 received in six years'
        time, at 16%)
    = −£16,100 + (£4,000 × 3.6847) + (£3,000 × 0.4014)
    = −£16,100 + £14,739 + £1,204
    = −£157

We now have one positive NPV result and one negative NPV
result, allowing us to use linear interpolation to estimate the IRR.
This can be represented graphically:

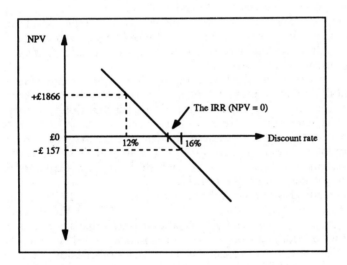

1. the distances between the two observed NPVs and the zero
NPV point (i.e. £1,866 and £157), and
2. the distances between the two trial discount rates and the IRR,
have the same ratio.

Interpolating between the 12% and 16% results we find that:

$$IRR = 12\% + \left[\frac{1,866}{1,866 - (-157)}\right] \times (16\% - 12\%)$$
$$= 12\% + (0.922 \times 4\%)$$
$$= \underline{15.69\%}$$

In Example 3.8 the IRR of 15.69% is much closer to 16% than to 12%, and this was obvious from the NPV results. The 12% calculation produced an answer that deviated by £1,866 from the desired zero point, while the 16% answer was only £157 off target.

It should be noted that linear interpolation provides only an estimate of IRR. "Linear" interpolation assumes that the relationship between the two data points is that of a straight line. This is rarely true. So, the closer are the two discount rates used, the more accurate will be the answer, as a straight line will better approximate the relationship over a shorter distance. For instance, in Example 3.8 a more accurate answer would have been obtained by interpolating between 15% and 16%. However, the degree of accuracy is often not crucial – the uncertainty inherent in the inputs to CI analysis means that IRR can only ever be an estimate. Also, with increasing access to computer IRR functions, manual interpolation is rarely required.

So, the IRR method, while using the same cashflow information as the NPV method, presents a percentage return of the investment, rather than measuring the investment's net contribution to wealth. The acceptance criterion then focuses on whether the IRR exceeds the investor's RRR. Research evidence suggests that many practitioners favour the percentage expression of IRR. However, the reasons for this preference (which is further explored in Chapter 6) may be of questionable validity.

There are also some weaknesses associated with IRR, arising both from its mathematical formulation, and from the model's inherent assumptions. The IRR equation requires that a polynomial root (or solution) can be found which makes the NPV equal to zero. However, there are cases where a series of cashflows has no root, or has multiple roots. Consider Examples 3.9 and 3.10:

EXAMPLE 3.9

Cashflows with no IRR solution

	Time 0	Yr 1	Yr 2
Cashflow	+£1,000	−£3,000	+£2,500

EXAMPLE 3.10

Cashflows with multiple IRR solutions

	Time 0	Yr 1	Yr 2
Cashflow	−£4,000	+£25,000	−£25,000

This set of cashflows has IRR solutions at 25% and 400%, and would produce a positive NPV at any discount rate between these two values.

In such cases, the use of IRR as a decision-support tool is problematic. Which IRR is the correct one? A necessary (but not sufficient) condition for multiple IRR solutions is that there is more than one change in the sign of the cashflows. Typically, we see an initial cash outflow, followed by a series of inflows over the life of the CI. However, as in Example 3.10, where there are further changes in the sign of the cashflows, the multiple solution problem can occur. Remember that an IRR is found where the NPV is equal to zero. Therefore if we graph a CI's NPV against a range of discount rates, we can see the points at which the graph intersects the x-axis (where NPV = 0). Example 3.11 illustrates this. In Example 3.11, where there is only one change in the sign of cashflows, we see a unidirectional function, such as A. However, for more than one change in sign, the graph changes direction and may reintercept the x-axis, as is the case for B. However, where there are *no* IRR solutions (as for C), any number of changes in sign may occur without an IRR being found. That is

EXAMPLE 3.11

Graphing the NPV/IRR relationship

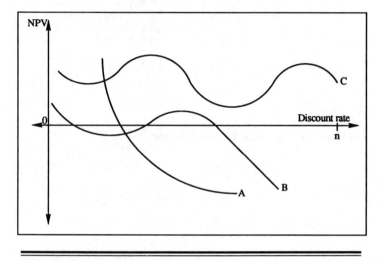

why we say that multiple changes in the sign of the cashflows are a necessary, but not sufficient, condition for multiple IRRs. However, the possibility of multiple IRRs makes the IRR method less attractive as a CI analysis tool. The second main problem with the IRR approach is that it can produce rankings of CI projects which conflict with those obtained using NPV. This becomes a problem where a firm must select between mutually exclusive CI projects. The problem can be illustrated using a simple example.

EXAMPLE 3.12

Conflicting project rankings using IRR and NPV

Commercial Co. owns a factory. It is considering investing in modifications to that factory, and must choose between two options with the following cashflows:

1. spend £40,000 now and receive £58,000 in three years' time, or
2. spend £40,000 now and receive £46,000 in one year's time.

This modification is a one-off expenditure, and no further investment opportunities are expected for at least four years.

Commercial Co. has a required rate of return of 10%.

Calculating the NPV and IRR of these two options, we get:

Project	NPV (@10%)	IRR
1	+£3,576	13.19%
2	+£1,818	15.00%

Therefore, using the NPV rule we would accept option 1 as it has the greater NPV. However, using the IRR rule (where both options exceed the RRR), we would be inclined to select option 2, as it has the greater IRR.

The difference in ranking results from the differing "reinvestment assumptions" (or in this case, perhaps better referred to as the "opportunity cost" assumptions) of the NPV and IRR approaches. If project 1 is forgone, the investor forfeits a return (for three years) of 13.19%. If project 2 is forgone, the investor forfeits a return (for one year) of 15%. While the IRR of project 2 appears more appealing, the NPV shows us that if we invest £40,000, a 15% return for one year is worth less than a 13.19% return for three years, where no subsequent investment opportunities are available.

It is not appropriate to use the IRR approach for ranking mutually exclusive projects. Clearly project 1 should be accepted, as it will make the larger contribution to the wealth of the investor. Reliance on the IRR rankings would lead to an incorrect decision in this instance. However, the IRR method can be adapted to overcome this conflicting rankings problem. Rather than considering the cashflows of each option separately, we can calculate the IRR of the *difference* between their cashflows. If the IRR of the incremental cashflows is greater than the required rate of return, then the lower IRR project is, in fact, the preferred option. We can illustrate this by reconsidering the two projects in Example 3.12.

EXAMPLE 3.13

Calculating the incremental IRR for project ranking

	Time 0	Yr 1	Yr 2	Yr 3
Cashflows:				
Option 1:	−£40,000	—	—	+£58,000
Option 2:	−£40,000	+£46,000	—	—
Difference:	—	−£46,000	—	+£58,000

The IRR of these cashflows can be found quite simply, by solving the equation:

$$0 = \frac{-£46,000}{(1 + IRR)} + \frac{+£58,000}{(1 + IRR)^3}$$

and works out to be 12.29%.[5] As this exceeds the RRR of 10%, option 1 – with the lower IRR – should be accepted. This was the conclusion that would have been reached under the NPV criterion.

So, it is not impossible to use IRR for ranking mutually exclusive projects. However, it is a cumbersome procedure, requiring several IRR computations, with much potential for confusion. Remember, the example shown here is extremely simplified. Imagine the problems involved in applying this procedure to a choice between many project options, all with multiple cashflows. The best advice would appear to be – use the NPV criterion!

A further problem with IRR is that it assumes that the RRR will be constant over the life of the CI. If changes in the RRR are anticipated, we can deal with this using the NPV approach by discounting each year's cashflow by the appropriate RRR for that year. However, with IRR this is not an option.

---

[5] The solution proceeds as follows:

$$\frac{46,000}{(1 + IRR)} = \frac{58,000}{(1 + IRR)^3}$$

$\Rightarrow \quad 46,000 \times (1 + IRR)^3 = 58,000 \times (1 + IRR)$

$\Rightarrow \quad (1 + IRR)^2 = 58,000 \div 46,000$

$\Rightarrow \quad (1 + IRR) = \sqrt{1.2609}$

$\Rightarrow \quad IRR = 12.29\%$

A final blow to the usefulness of IRR arises from its implicit reinvestment assumption. The IRR model assumes that all cashflows produced by a CI can be reinvested at the IRR. This is often unrealistic. If a project has an IRR of 20 per cent but market rates for investment are only 14 per cent, then we cannot expect to reinvest cashflows arising from the CI at the 20 per cent rate. So, the IRR method has overstated the return which will realistically be generated by the CI. It is more likely that we will be reinvesting resultant cashflows at a rate something like our RRR, or cost of capital. Using NPV no such assumption is required as it is possible to vary discount rates to reflect changing investment possibilities over the life of the project. So here again, the NPV approach is preferred.

A step in the right direction: discounted payback period

When the payback period (PP) method was considered earlier, it was noted that a variation called the "discounted payback period" (DPP) improved this approach. The DPP approach has all the perceived advantages of PP – it is easy to understand and compute, and it allows the investor to focus on liquidity where this is appropriate. But, unlike PP, DPP takes into account the time value of money. Therefore, the DPP approach is a useful step towards the theoretically superior method of NPV, particularly for smaller business managers who find the PP approach attractive.

The DPP method discounts each year's net cashflow by the appropriate discount rate and determines the number of years it takes for these discounted cashflows to recoup the CI's initial outlay. Because DPP recognizes the time value of money, it produces a longer payback period than does the non-discounted PP approach, and takes into account more of the CI's cashflows. Another advantage of DPP over the traditional PP method is that it has a clear accept-or-reject criterion. Using DPP, a project is acceptable if it pays back within its lifetime. Example 3.14 illustrates the difference between the PP and DPP approaches.

EXAMPLE 3.14

Payback period v. discounted payback period

An investment with an initial outlay of £20,000, produces net cash inflows of £7,000 p.a. for six years.

Year	Net cashflow (£)	Present value (@ 15%)	Cumulative present value (£)
0	−20,000	−20,000	−20,000
1	+7,000	+6,087	−13,913
2	+7,000	+5,293	−8,620
3	+7,000	+4,603	−4,017
4	+7,000	+4,002	−15
5	+7,000	+3,480	+3,465
6	+7,000	+3,026	+6,491

Accept the investment?

PP : the payback period is just under three years (£20,000 ÷ £7,000). Acceptance depends on the arbitrarily determined cut-off time: if cut-off is two years, reject; if three years, accept.

DPP: the discounted payback period is just over four years. The investment would be accepted, as it pays back within its six-year lifetime.

Discounted payback period still shares one limitation with PP: cashflows which occur after the payback period are ignored. However, since the DPP is always longer than the PP, the DPP method ignores fewer of these cashflows. DPP also conveys a sense of liquidity measurement which is not achieved using the NPV method. For example, to a cash-constrained business, a DPP of three years would be more attractive than a DPP of five years. Since PP is often the only CI analysis undertaken in smaller businesses, switching to DPP is a step in the right direction.

THE WINNER: NPV

The economics-derived discounted cashflow (DCF) methods (NPV, PI, IRR and to a lesser extent, DPP) provide the most convincing link between CI analysis and the assumed objective of the firm − maximization of wealth. Payback period is a useful first screening device, and AROR has some strength in facilitating comparison of CI outcomes with the profit measures for which decision-makers are often held accountable. But only the DCF methods focus, as the name suggests, on cash (the source of wealth) and the time value of money (the value of that cash). The question now is, which DCF method is best?

By now it will be clear that the apparent similarity between the IRR and NPV approaches is only skin-deep! Although they both use discounted cashflows, IRR has several characteristics which make it difficult to use, and misleading, under some commonly encountered conditions. Although the IRR approach can be adapted to overcome some of these deficiencies, it is much easier instead to use the NPV analysis method.

NPV has none of the computational problems of IRR, and further, it indicates the value which a CI has to the investor. After all, how much is an IRR of (say) 16 per cent worth? It may be a small fortune if the investment is £1 million, but it may be insignificant if the investment is £1! Much better to know how much better off the CI will make the investor, and a combination of NPV and PI can tell us both the value of the CI, and the significance of that return relative to the size of the investment. The NPV also allows for additivity of CI values, where IRRs cannot be added to achieve a sense of the total return to the organization.

So, IRR *can* work (but sometimes doesn't and is complex), DPP is a step in the right direction, and NPV is best! Now that we know why NPV is preferred, there are some issues that must be addressed to ensure that it is used correctly. These issues are considered in the next chapter.

Suggestions for further reading

Lumby, S. (1991). *Investment Appraisal and Financing Decisions* (4th edn.), Chapman & Hall, London.

Northcott, D. (1991). "Capital investment for small business", *Accounting Forum (Aust.)*, Vol. 14 (4), March, pp. 84–97.

Pike, R.H. (1985). "Disenchantment with DCF promotes IRR", *Certified Accountant*, July, pp. 14–17.

Problems

1. Outline the main features of the following CI analysis methods, identifying their relative strengths and weaknesses:
   a. payback period
   b. discounted payback period
   c. accounting rate of return
   d. internal rate of return
   e. net present value
   f. profitability index.
2. What is a "sunk cost"? How should sunk costs be treated in the analysis of CI projects?

3. Outline the main differences between the "accounting"
    perspective on CI analysis, and the "economics"-type
    approach. Comment on the relevance of these two perspectives
    for CI decision-making.
4. What are the factors that contribute to the "time value of
    money"? Why is the time value of money concept relevant
    to CI decision-making?
5. Westend Co. is evaluating two CI projects. These projects
    are mutually exclusive as they would both use the same
    currently vacant floorspace, although there is no capital
    rationing constraint.

	Project J	*Project K*
Time 0	£20,000	£40,000
Year 1	£10,000	£20,000
Year 2	£10,000	£20,000
Year 3	£10,000	£20,000

Westend usually uses the IRR approach to assessing CI
projects, with a 16% minimum required rate of return.
Required:
(a) Calculate the IRRs and NPVs of Project J and Project K.
(b) Explain the difficulties of using the IRR approach for
    selecting between these two projects.
(c) Suggest an alternative approach which will satisfy the
    company's desire to use the IRR method while improving
    the decision results achieved. Recalculate the relevant IRR
    figures using this approach to demonstrate its advantages.
6. The managers of O'Doolin Co. have traditionally used
    payback period and accounting rate of return criteria for
    assessing CI projects. They consider a project to be acceptable
    if it pays back within four years, and has an AROR of at
    least 20%. The following information relates to a CI
    opportunity currently under consideration (ignore taxation).

Year	Net cashflow produced	Depreciation expense
0	−£28,000	nil
1	+£10,000	£3,000
2	+£ 8,000	£3,000
3	+£ 7,000	£3,000
4	+£ 5,000	£3,000
5	+£ 3,000	£3,000

The project will have a salvage value of £6,000 at the end of year 5.

(a) Calculate the project's payback period.

(b) Calculate the project's accounting rate of return using:
    (i) the "initial investment" denominator, and
    (ii) the "average investment" denominator.

(c) Would this project be acceptable to O'Doolin Co.?

(d) You suggest to the managers of O'Doolin Co. that the discounted payback period method would produce an improved analysis. On the basis of this criterion (using a 14% required rate of return), would you recommend that the CI project be undertaken? Show your calculations.

7.   Sayer Co. is considering signing a contract with an advertising agency to promote one of its products, Scented Body Lotion. The advertising agency requires immediate payment of £6,000, plus an annual payment of £2,000 at the end of each of the next three years. The advertising agency predicts that the Scented Body Lotion campaign will increase sales of this product by 3000 units per annum for the next three years (while the campaign continues). Also, long-term effects from improved consumer awareness are expected to produce increased sales of 1000 units per annum for the following three years. Each unit of Scented Body Lotion sold contributes a positive cashflow of £1.50, and it is assumed that these cashflows accrue at the end of each year of sales. Ignore taxation and inflation and assume that Sayer Co. has a 16% required rate of return for its cosmetic products.

(a) Calculate for the advertising campaign:
    (i) its payback period
    (ii) its discounted payback period
    (iii) its net present value, and
    (iv) its profitability index.

(b) Would you recommend signing the advertising contract?
Why, or why not?

(c) What other uncertain factors might you wish to investigate
before making such an investment decision?

8. The Marlborough Meat Co. is required by new hygiene
regulations to install stainless steel flooring in its processing
area. It is considering three options, all of which have an
expected useful life of ten years in meeting required hygiene
standards:

Option 1 – low grade flooring:	initial cost = £15,000
	annual maintenance costs = £3,000
	annual cleaning costs = £4,000
Option 2 – medium grade flooring:	initial cost = £18,000
	annual maintenance costs = £2,000
	annual cleaning costs = £2,000
Option 3 – high grade flooring:	initial cost = £24,000
	annual maintenance costs = £1,000
	annual cleaning costs = £2,000

Using an NPV analysis (with a 14% opportunity cost of
capital), which option would you recommend to Marlborough
Meat Co.?

4

Using NPV Correctly: Some Further Issues

It has been established that NPV is the theoretically superior, and least problematic, approach to financially analysing CI proposals. However, there are practical aspects of undertaking NPV analyses that must be considered if the financial assessment of CIs is to be sound. This chapter will explore several of these practical issues and outline appropriate approaches to incorporating them in the NPV analysis.

TAXATION

Up until now, for simplicity, we have ignored the effects of taxation. In reality, tax has a significant impact on the cashflows of CIs. Where cashflows from a CI change the amount of tax payable, then this is itself a real cashflow effect. There are a number of ways in which these tax effects occur:

- when revenues (or reduced costs) from a CI increase profit
- when costs (or reduced revenues) of a CI decrease profit
- when a gain or loss is made on the sale of a fixed asset
- when a CI is depreciated or written down
- when special taxation relief is provided as an investment incentive.

Costs and revenues

The first of these taxation effects are perhaps the most obvious. It is unrealistic to consider only pre-tax cash revenues from a CI, as revenues which change reported profits also change tax liabilities. Therefore, any cashflows which affect reported profit will produce a corresponding taxation cashflow.

The next point to consider is the timing of these tax cashflows. Most businesses pay tax one year after the end of each financial year. So, a cost or revenue which occurs *now* produces a taxation effect one year after the end of the current financial year. Of course, CI cashflows may occur at any time during the year; we frequently deal with this by employing the simplifying assumption that all cashflows occur at the end of the year.

However, if a cashflow is known to occur close to the start of a financial period, it is more realistic to recognize that the tax effect will occur in about two years' time (the end of the financial period is one year away, and the tax effect occurs one year after that). In practice, treatment of cashflow timing in CI analysis usually requires an element of approximation. As the cashflows are rarely certain, simplifying assumptions about their timing do not usually present a problem.

Example 4.1 provides a simple illustration of tax calculation and timing effects.

EXAMPLE 4.1

Tax effect on CI costs and revenues

Hanson Co. is considering purchasing a new packaging machine. The machine will cost £40,000 and installation costs will be £2,000. A £3,000 increase in inventory will be required, which can be liquidated for £3,000 at the end of the machine's five-year life. The machine is expected to cost £20,000 p.a. to run, but will reduce packaging costs by an estimated £40,000 p.a. It will have a zero salvage value in five years' time. Hanson Co. is subject to a 35% tax rate.

Calculating tax cashflows
Only the increased costs and revenues appear in the income statement, affecting profit and therefore tax. Both the asset price and installation cost are capitalized to the asset account, and the increased inventory is a current asset, rather than an expense.

So, the relevant cashflows are:

	Time 0	Yr 1	Yr 2	Yr 3	Yr 4	Yr 5	Yr 6
Cashflows:							
Purchase price	−£40,000						
Installation	£2,000						
Inventory	−£3,000					+£3,000	
Running costs		−£20,000	−£20,000	−£20,000	−£20,000	−£20,000	
Cost savings		+£40,000	+£40,000	+£40,000	+£40,000	+£40,000	
Increased tax*			−£7,000	−£7,000	−£7,000	−£7,000	−£7,000
TOTALS	−£45,000	+£20,000	+£13,000	+£13,000	+£13,000	+£16,000	−£7,000

* The tax effect is calculated as: (increase in profit) × (tax rate)

$$= (£40,000 - £20,000) \times 0.35$$
$$= £7,000$$

As profit has *increased*, so will the tax liability, producing a cash *outflow*, assumed to occur one year after the costs and revenues themselves.

Gains or losses on asset sales

If a CI project involves the sale of a currently held asset, further taxation effects can occur. If the selling price differs from the asset's net book value then a gain or loss on sale occurs. Although not actual cashflows in themselves, gains will increase profit, thus increasing tax, and losses will decrease profit and reduce tax payable. These changes to the tax liability are known as balancing charges (where tax liability increases) and balancing allowances (where a loss on sale reduces tax).

Balancing allowances are only realizable where the investor (or organization) has a tax liability for the year, against which the allowance can be offset. Normally, where this is the case, the tax effect will occur one year after the end of the financial period in which the asset sale was made.[1] Sometimes, where there is no current tax liability, balancing allowances can be carried forward

---

[1] This tax effect, like all others, depends on the relative timing of the end of the financial tax period, so simplifying assumptions are often required.

to a future tax period in which a tax liability does exist. Example 4.2 illustrates the possible tax effects where an asset is sold.

EXAMPLE 4.2

Tax effects from the sale of an asset

Angle Co. is considering replacing an old forklift purchased six years ago for £50,000 with an estimated useful life of ten years. It has been depreciated on a straight-line basis to a salvage value of £10,000. Angle Co. has a 35% tax rate.

Calculating the net book value of the forklift

Book value = original purchase price − accumulated depreciation

$$= £50,000 \quad - \quad \left[6 \times \frac{(£50,000 - £10,000)}{10} \right]$$

$$= \underline{£26,000}$$

Selling price scenarios

1. *The old forklift is sold for £30,000 (cash received now):*

$$
\begin{aligned}
\text{gain on sale} &= (£30,000 - £26,000) \\
&= £4,000 \\
\Rightarrow \quad \text{Balancing charge} &= £4,000 \times 0.35 \\
&= \underline{£1,400} \text{ (tax } payable \text{ in one year's time)}
\end{aligned}
$$

2. *The old forklift is sold for £15,000 (cash received now):*

$$
\begin{aligned}
\text{loss on sale} &= (£26,000 - £15,000) \\
&= £11,000 \\
\Rightarrow \quad \text{Balancing allowance} &= £11,000 \times 0.35 \\
&= \underline{£3,850} \text{ (tax } credit \text{ received in one year's time)}
\end{aligned}
$$

So, when the sale of an existing asset forms part of a CI proposal, both the cash received for the asset (i.e. its selling price) and the taxation implications of any gain or loss on sale must be taken into account in analysing the cashflows.

Depreciation/writing down allowances

Although the purchase price of a CI is incurred at the outset of the investment, financial accounting practice is to spread this initial cost over the life of an asset via depreciation. Depreciation is designed to reflect (for accounting purposes) the fact that the benefit from a CI accrues over a number of years, and so its cost is "matched" to that benefit by recognizing a proportion of the asset's outlay each year.

When conducting NPV analysis, depreciation itself is meaningless. The initial cash outlay occurs at "time 0", and the accounting treatment of the asset does not change that. However, as an asset is depreciated over its life, that depreciation is recognized as an expense in the income statement each year, thus reducing profit. And as we know, a reduction in profit, though looking bad from an accounting point of view, is good from a cashflow perspective, as it means less tax!

Different countries have different ways of allowing asset depreciation for taxation purposes. Some countries prescribe allowable depreciation rates which a business can use to expense assets in the income statement. Other countries (like the UK) have replaced depreciation tax allowances with "writing down allowances" (WDAs) which are established at a fixed rate. The current UK system is to allow a 25 per cent WDA, based on the diminishing value of the capital asset.

Normally, the first WDA takes effect one year after the purchase of the CI. But complications arise, depending on the stage of the financial tax year at which the asset is purchased. For example, if an asset is purchased on the last day of a financial year, and has an expected life of five years, it will qualify for six WDAs. This is because the first WDA is allowed for the year in which it is purchased, even if it was only owned for one day of that year. So, the first WDA is allowable immediately, and the first tax benefit of this will accrue in one year's time. The asset will have a further five years' life (and five WDAs) remaining.

If, on the other hand, the asset is purchased on the first day of the financial year, its first WDA does not accrue until the end of the year – in one year's time. So, the tax effect is two years away. Also, the asset creates one less WDA, as its life extends over only five financial periods. Clearly, if the option is available to the investor, it is better to invest in a CI a day earlier, if it means it will squeak into the end of a financial year! It makes very little difference to the timing of the outlay, but the result is one more WDA and a faster start to the series of tax benefits. Example 4.3 shows WDA calculations and taxation effects.

EXAMPLE 4.3

WDAs and their taxation effects

An asset is purchased by Taylor Co. for £100,000, and has a useful life of four years. It is subject to a writing down allowance of 25% (on its diminishing value). Taylor Co. is subject to a 35% tax rate.

WDA allowances

		Tax effect (cash inflow)
1st WDA	£100,000 × 0.25 = £25,000	£25,000 × 0.35 = £8,750
2nd WDA	£75,000 × 0.25 = £18,750	£18,750 × 0.35 = £6,563
3rd WDA	£56,250 × 0.25 = £14,063	£14,063 × 0.35 = £4,922
4th WDA	£42,187 × 0.25 = £10,547	£10,547 × 0.35 = £3,691
5th WDA*	£31,640 × 0.25 = £ 7,910	£ 7,910 × 0.35 = £2,769

* The fifth WDA only accrues under scenario 2.

Scenario 1 – it is the first day of the financial year

	Time 0	Yr 1	Yr 2	Yr 3	Yr 4	Yr 5
Cashflows:						
Initial outlay	−£100,000					
WDA tax effects		−	+£8,750	+£6,563	+£4,922	+£3,691

Scenario 2 – it is the last day of the financial year

	Time 0	Yr 1	Yr 2	Yr 3	Yr 4	Yr 5
Cashflows:						
Initial outlay	−£100,000					
WDA tax effects		+£8,750	+£6,563	+£4,922	+£3,691	+£2,769

It is clear from Example 4.3 that the CI decision-maker should, where possible, arrange the timing of CI asset purchases to take best advantage of taxation allowances. Delaying purchase for only one day can be expensive, simply by impacting upon the tax liability of the business.

Taxation investment incentives

Sometimes governments make special taxation provisions to encourage investment in particular types of capital asset. In these cases, writing down allowances may be accelerated, or there may be special "one-off" tax credits in the year of the asset's purchase. It is in the interests of the CI decision-maker to be aware of such incentives, as they could have a significant impact on the viability of a CI project.

Taxation effects: summary

Taxation affects the NPV of a CI by changing its cashflows. This occurs because real cash effects of a CI (e.g. revenues and costs) and the accounting treatment of CI effects (e.g. gains and losses on asset sale and depreciation/WDAs) all impact on reported profit, and therefore change tax liabilities. A CI proposal cannot be analysed correctly without taking into account these taxation issues.

INFLATION

Inflation affects the value of cashflows arising from a CI by eroding their purchasing power. As indicated in the previous chapter in the introduction to "the time value of money", market interest rates include an "expectation of inflation". That is, investors want to be compensated for the reduced purchasing power of future cashflows due to inflation, so inflation is built into the required rate of return. Similarly, inflation is often implicitly "absorbed" into RRRs used for the assessment of CIs.

A rate of return which includes an inflation component is called a *nominal* rate. We can also determine the *real* rate of return (i.e. with the inflation component removed), as illustrated in Example 4.4.

EXAMPLE 4.4

Nominal and real rates of return

A firm expects continuing inflation of 6%. In setting their nominal required rate of return on CIs, they want to be compensated for this inflation effect, plus they want the investment to return an 8% real return.

$$(1 + \text{nominal RRR}) = (1 + \text{real RRR}) \times (1 + \text{inflation rate})$$
$$= (1 + 0.08) \times (1 + 0.06)$$
$$= (1.1448)$$

So, the firm's nominal RRR is 14.48%. This means that it has produced a real wealth increase of 8% after taking into account the erosive effects of inflation.

Note that it is incorrect to simply add the real RRR to the inflation rate. Inflation is a multiplier effect; i.e. a cashflow must multiply by (1 + inflation rate) each year in order to retain the same purchasing power. We can generalize the relationship between real and nominal RRRs in two ways:

$$\text{Real rate} = \frac{(1 + \text{nominal rate})}{(1 + \text{inflation rate})} - 1$$

and

$$\text{Nominal rate} = [(1 + \text{real rate}) \times (1 + \text{inflation rate})] - 1$$

It is important to distinguish between real and nominal RRRs when discounting cashflows for NPV analysis. Both the rate and the cashflows used must be consistent. Therefore, if a nominal RRR is used as the discount rate, then it should be recognized that inflation will increase the nominal size of the cashflows over the life of the CI. On the other hand, if cashflows are assumed to stay constant over the life of the asset, then a real RRR should be used. It is a common mistake to use inconsistent combinations of RRRs and cashflows, resulting in incorrect NPV analyses.

Since there are two approaches, the next question is which one is best? This has an "it depends" response. The advantage of using a nominal RRR in combination with inflated cashflows is that we can recognize that not all costs and revenues inflate at the same rate. For example, we may expect a 6 per cent general inflation rate, but may expect that the cost of labour will inflate at 8 per cent per annum. By inflating each type of cashflow separately we can recognize this. So, if the information is available for this approach, then the nominal RRR/inflated cashflow approach gives a better reflection of the true value of future cashflows.

However, it is often difficult to forecast specific price indices for individual cost and revenue items, and the general price index is often used as a surrogate. Of course, use of a general inflation index assumes that all cashflows inflate at the same rate, and so the advantage of the nominal RRR/inflated cashflow approach disappears. Using a general inflation rate, the same NPV result will occur using this method as would be achieved by using real cashflows and a real (inflation-adjusted) RRR. Example 4.5 illustrates the two approaches.

EXAMPLE 4.5

Discounting using real and nominal RRRs

Dixon Co. has a nominal RRR of 20%, at a time where there is an 8% inflation expectation. They want to undertake NPV analysis on the following project:

- initial outlay = £50,000
- life of the project = four years (zero salvage value)
- current estimation of after-tax cash savings from the project = £30,000 p.a.

1. *Using nominal RRR and nominal cashflows:*

Inflated cashflows: Yr 1 = (£30,000 × 1.08) = £32,400
Yr 2 = (£30,000 × 1.08²) = £34,992
Yr 3 = (£30,000 × 1.08³) = £37,791
Yr 4 = (£30,000 × 1.08⁴) = £40,815

$$\text{NPV} = (-£50,000) + \frac{£32,400}{(1.20)} + \frac{£34,992}{(1.20)^2} + \frac{£37,791}{(1.20)^3} + \frac{£40,815}{(1.20)^4}$$

= −£50,000 + £27,000 + £24,300 + £21,870 + £19,683

= +£42,853

2. *Using real RRR and real cashflows:*
Real RRR = [(1.20) ÷ (1.08)] − 1
= 11.11%

$$\text{NPV} = (-£50,000) + \frac{£30,000}{(1.1111)} + \frac{£30,000}{(1.1111)^2} + \frac{£30,000}{(1.1111)^3} + \frac{£30,000}{(1.1111)^4}$$

= −£50,000 + £27,000 + £24,300 + £21,871 + £19,684

= £42,855

(The two solutions differ by £2 due to rounding effects).

Whether specific or general price indices are used to adjust for inflation, the most important requirement is that the RRR used as a discount rate is consistent with the approach used for determining the CI's cashflows.

COMPARING PROJECTS WITH UNEQUAL LIVES

Where projects are mutually exclusive, choosing between them becomes more difficult where they have unequal lives. It is not appropriate to simply compare the NPVs of the projects, as it is not realistic to compare, say a five-year option with a ten-year option. The shorter-life option may need more frequent replacement, or may free up funds for alternative investment elsewhere. Therefore, we must somehow put the projects on an "equal footing" so that an appropriate comparison can be made. There are three ways of doing this:

1. Finding a common multiple of the years of life of each investment and assuming that each project self-replaces until a common time-horizon is reached (e.g. comparing two five-year project iterations to one ten-year project).
2. Using the "equivalent annual cashflows" approach.
3. Making a simplifying assumption that the longer-life project is sold at a time corresponding to the life of the shorter investment, and taking its terminal value into account in the NPV calculation.

Example 4.6 illustrates the three alternative approaches.

_____

EXAMPLE 4.6

Comparing projects with unequal lives

Koh Co. wishes to compare two mutually exclusive projects, using a 16% RRR:

  Project A: Invest £30,000 now, get £15,000 p.a. for six years
  Project B: Invest £20,000 now, get £18,000 p.a. for three years

Calculating their NPVs

Project A = −£30,000 + (annuity of £15,000 for six years at 16%)
      = −£30,000 + (£15,000 × 3.6847)
      = +£25,271

Project B = −£20,000 + (annuity of £18,000 for three years at
16%)

= −£20,000 + (£18,000 × 2.2459)

= +£20,426

Therefore, on NPVs alone, the initial reaction may be to select project A. But:

1. *Assume replacement of project B*

$$NPV = -£20,000 + \frac{£18,000}{(1.16)} + \frac{£18,000}{(1.16)^2} + \frac{£18,000 - £20,000}{(1.16)^3}$$

$$+ \frac{£18,000}{(1.16)^4} + \frac{£18,000}{(1.16)^5} + \frac{£18,000}{(1.16)^6}$$

$$= +£33,511$$

The NPV of two iterations of project B exceeds that of project A, so accept B.

2. *Use equivalent annual cashflows*

This method determines the annuity which, over the life of each investment, would produce the investment's NPV. This is obtained by dividing the project's NPV by the annuity factor appropriate to the RRR and the life of the investment. The project with the greater annuity equivalent is offering the best return and should be selected.

Project A: equivalent annual cashflow = NPV ÷ (annuity factor for six years at 16%)

⇒ e.a.cf. = +£25,271 ÷ 3.6847

= +£6,858

Project B:

e.a.cf. = +£20,426 ÷ (annuity factor for three years at 16%)

= +£20,426 ÷ 2.2459

= +£9,095

Therefore project B is preferred, as it represents an equivalent annual cashflow greater than that offered by project A.

3. *Assume a terminal value for project A at the end of year 3*

Let us say that we can estimate the terminal/sales value of project A at the end of year 3 as £15,000. We can now shorten the time period over which project A is assessed to match that for project B:

NPV(A) = −£30,000 + (annuity of £15,000 for three years at 16%)
            + (present value of the terminal value of £15,000 in
            three years' time at 16%)
      = −£30,000 + (£15,000 × 2.2459) + (£15,000 × 0.6407)
      = +£13,299

So again, project B would be selected as it has the higher NPV.

Of the approaches detailed above, the equivalent annual cashflow is the more technically correct, and is generally easy to use. But, where project lives have an obvious common multiple, replacement assumption may be appropriate. Finally, where the project lives are long, it is often sufficient to assume a terminal value for the longer-life project, as the distance of the cashflows reduces the impact of their discounted values.

The important thing is to ensure that erroneous choices are not made by looking only at projects' NPVs where differing project lives make this an inappropriate comparison.

CAPITAL RATIONING

It has been assumed up to this point that a firm will have sufficient funds available to invest in any available project which has a positive NPV. However, due to externally imposed restrictions, (hard capital rationing) or internally imposed budgets (soft capital rationing) funds available to the firm for investment may be limited. Where this is the case, a choice must be made between positive NPV projects.

Here, the profitability index (PI) is more useful than the NPV measure. While NPV shows the value of an investment, PI expresses that value as a proportion of the initial outlay funds required. Therefore, where funds are scarce, a higher PI project would be preferred as it returns more per scarce pound than a project with a lower PI. Example 4.7 illustrates project selection under capital rationing conditions.

EXAMPLE 4.7

Project selection under capital rationing conditions

Mills Co. has £100,000 available for capital investment in the current period. They have the following CI projects available:

Project	Initial outlay	NPV	PI
A	£50,000	£80,000	1.6
B	£30,000	£45,000	1.5
C	£20,000	£40,000	2.0
D	£30,000	£42,000	1.4
E	£20,000	£32,000	1.6

Ranking these projects in order of PI, projects C, A and E would be undertaken, with the remaining £10,000 available put towards project B. This would produce a total NPV of [£40,000 + £80,000 + £32,000 + (£45,000 ÷ 3)] = £167,000.

A basic assumption here is that projects are divisible (as with project B above). This may not always be the case in practice, and not all available funds may be spent, if only "whole" projects are selected. If faced with non–divisible projects, different groupings of projects may be possible, which meet the budget allowance for expenditure. Here the investor must treat the projects as a portfolio, selecting the portfolio which produces the highest total NPV addition to wealth. Consider Example 4.8, using the project opportunities in Example 4.7.

EXAMPLE 4.8

The "portfolio" approach to selecting projects under capital rationing

Possible project groupings:

Project combination	NPVs (£000)	Total NPV (£000)
A,B,C	80 + 45 + 40	165
A,B,E	80 + 45 + 32	157
A,C,D	80 + 40 + 42	162
A,C,E	80 + 40 + 32	152
A,D,E	80 + 42 + 32	154
B,C,D,E	45 + 40 + 42 + 32	159

So, where project B cannot be partially undertaken, the preferred combination of projects changes to A, B and C. This produces a total NPV of £165,000, which is less than the total of £167,000 which would have been possible if project B were divisible (as in Example 4.7 above).

So generally, under conditions of capital rationing, selecting those projects with the largest PIs will produce the best overall NPV to the firm. However, where projects are non-divisible, a "portfolio" approach is needed to select the best feasible project combination, although the constraint of non-divisibility will often mean that the overall NPV is reduced.

A more sophisticated approach to selecting CI projects under conditions of single or multi-period capital rationing is the use of linear programming (LP). Linear programming is (usually) a computerized mathematical technique from the operations research literature. It calculates optimal solutions where an objective (e.g. maximizing NPV) is pursued under constrained conditions (e.g. capital rationing). In its more sophisticated forms it can cope with probabilistic outcomes, multiple objectives and multiple constraints. Linear programming is also useful where minimum liquidity and profitability constraints must be met by a CI investment programme.

To use LP the CI decision-maker must be able to formulate an "objective function" and "constraint functions" which quantify the relevant information to the CI decision. Therefore, this approach can be complex to use, requiring relatively strong mathematical skills and a clear quantification of decision variables. However, it is the most sophisticated approach to dealing with capital rationing and is a valuable decision support tool for the CI decision-maker.

Let us consider a simple example of how LP can be used to

choose between competing CI projects where multi-period capital rationing exists. Example 4.9 provides an illustration.

EXAMPLE 4.9

A simple LP exercise under multi-period capital rationing conditions

A company has three potential CI projects. The NPVs of these projects (all positive) have been calculated, and are shown below. However, the company is restricted from undertaking all these projects by limited funding availability. This year and next year only £200,000 p.a. will be available for CI expenditure, and unspent amounts cannot be carried forward. The funding demands of the available CI projects are also shown below.

Project	NPV (£000s)	Cash input required (£000s):	
		This year	Next year
X	+180	60	80
Y	+370	100	100
Z	+540	140	140

The possible combinations of projects X, Y and Z can be identified, and the total ensuing NPV result calculated. However, not all these potential combinations are feasible, due to the £200,000 p.a. spending constraint. A summary of this information is given below.

Combinations	Total NPV (£000s)	Capital required (£000s):		Feasible?
		This year	Next year	
X alone	+180	60	80	Yes
Y alone	+370	100	100	Yes
Z alone	+540	140	140	Yes
X and Y	+550	160	180	Yes
X and Z	+720	200	220	No
Y and Z	+910	240	240	No
X, Y and Z	+1090	300	320	No

Note that, if only this year was considered, the combination of X and Z would be selected (total capital required is £200,000 and the total NPV is £720,000). However, since there is also a capital constraint *next year*, the X and Z combination would exceed this (total capital required is £220,000). So, the best option which is feasible over both years is the X and Y combination, with a total NPV of £550,000.

To formulate this problem as an LP problem, the following inputs would be required:

1. *Objective function*   Maximize 180 X + 370 Y + 540 Z (total NPV)
2. *Constraints*   Subject to:
    60 X + 100 Y + 140 Z ≤ 200 (£ this year)
    80 X + 100 Y + 140 Z ≤ 200 (£ next year)

Also, it is necessary to impose requirements so that the LP answers remain sensible. Therefore, solutions must either be 0 or 1. That is, there cannot be negative solutions (since we cannot "invest" negative amounts in a project), solutions must be whole numbers (since we cannot invest in "part" of a project) and solutions cannot exceed 1 (since we cannot invest more than once in the same project). Therefore, an *integer* constraint is required, where $0 \leq x \leq 1$ (x is the solution).

Once this formulated problem is solved by an LP computer program,[2] the output looks like this:

Summary of results			
Variables		Solution	Objective function coefficient
No.	Name		
1	X	+1.000	+180.000
2	Y	+1.000	+370.000
3	Z	0	+540.000
Maximum value of the objective = + 550.000			
Total iterations = 9			

[2] For this example the QSB (Quantitative Systems for Business) package was used.

This indicates that the optimal solution is to undertake one of project X, one of project Y and none of project Z. The resulting NPV (objective) would be +£550,000. The LP program also indicates that it required nine iterations in order to obtain this optimal solution.

So, the LP output agrees with the previous consideration of all possible project combinations. For such a simple example, there is little advantage in undertaking the LP procedure. However, it does demonstrate the workings of LP and its potential benefits where a number of projects are considered, subject to multiple constraints.

USING NPV: SUMMARY

"Real world" complications make the financial analysis of CI projects difficult. However, once the impact of these factors is assessed, the NPV analysis method (together with PI) can accommodate the effects of tax, depreciation and inflation and lead to correct decision-making where mutually exclusive projects exist. Linear programming (LP) is also a useful tool where CI occurs under constraints of capital availability, mutual exclusivity of projects, or liquidity and profitability requirements. As with most financial decision-making, the hard part is predicting what the future holds, but no CI analysis method alone can address this problem!

Now that we have explored the ways in which financial information can be correctly incorporated into the NPV model, we must consider another important aspect of this approach. What discount rate, or required rate of return (RRR), should we use? The next chapter considers RRR determination, and the implications of risk in CI projects.

Suggestions for further reading

Charles, I. (1989). "Linear programming: The basic steps", *Accountancy (UK)*, Vol. 104 (1152), August, pp. 85–7.

Fogler, H.R. (1972). "Ranking techniques and capital budgeting", *Accounting Review*, Vol. 47 (1), January, pp. 134–43.

Hodder, J.E. and Riggs, H.E. (1985). "Pitfalls in evaluating risky projects", *Harvard Business Review*, January–February, pp. 128–35.

Horngren, C.T. and Foster, G. (1991). *Cost Accounting: A Managerial Emphasis* (7th edn.), Prentice-Hall International, Englewood Cliffs, N.J. (Chapter 22).

Trivol, G.W. and McDaniel, W.R. (1987). "Uncertainty, capital immo-
bility and capital rationing in the investment decision", *Journal of
Business Finance and Accounting*, Vol. 14 (2), Summer, pp. 215–28.

Problems

1. Explain the difference between a *nominal* cashflow and a *real*
    cashflow.
2. During a period when the general rate of inflation is 6 per
    cent, the market interest rate is 15 per cent. What is the *real*
    interest rate?
3   Explain how the timing of the purchase of a capital asset, and
    subsequent taxation effects, can impact on the asset's NPV.
4. Miller Industries Ltd. bought a lathe for £8,000 five years
    ago, on the first day of the financial year. The lathe has been
    subject to an annual writing down allowance of 25 per cent
    on its diminishing value. If the lathe is now to be sold for
    £3,000, what cashflows will be associated with the asset sale?
5. Belcher Co. owns a disused machine which was purchased
    ten years ago for £45,000 and has a current written-down
    value of £8,000. There are two options available for this
    machine:
    (a) it can be sold to a scrap merchant for £6,000 payable
        immediately
    (b) it can be modified at an immediate cost of £14,000.
    If the machine is modified, it is expected to become productive
    immediately and will generate an after-tax cashflow of
    +£5,000 per annum for the next four years. The cost of
    modifying the machine would be capitalized and added on to
    its current written-down value. Writing down allowances of
    25 per cent per annum (on the machine's diminishing value)
    would then apply for the remaining four years of the modified
    machine's life.
    Belcher Co. is subject to a 35 per cent taxation rate, and uses
    a required rate of return of 14 per cent.
    (a) Identify the relevant cashflows for each of the alternative
        machine options (hint – don't forget about tax effects on
        non-cash items).
    (b) Calculate the NPV of each option (assume it is nearly the
        end of Belcher Co.'s financial year).
    (c) What course of action would you recommend?
6. Flamingo Co. has the opportunity to invest in a new machine.

They have determined the following information related to this investment:

- initial purchase price of machine = £100,000
- expected life = ten years
- expected salvage value = £20,000
- annual pre-tax running costs = £10,000
- annual pre-tax increase in revenue due to the new machine's capacity = £50,000
- required increase in raw materials inventory = £10,000 (expected to be liquidated at the end of the asset's life for £15,000)
- co. tax rate = 35 per cent
- writing down allowance on fixed assets = 25 per cent on diminishing value.

The company's after-tax real required rate of return is 7 per cent. Assume it is near the end of Flamingo Co.'s financial year.

Required:

(a) Calculate the amount and timing of the cashflows associated with the asset's annual running costs and revenues.

(b) Calculate the amount and timing of the cashflows associated with the writing down allowance on the asset.

(c) Incorporating all the relevant information, what is the investment's net present value?

(d) Based on your calculations in (c) above, would you recommend purchasing the machine?

(e) Assume now that Flamingo Co.'s *nominal* required rate of return is 20 per cent. What is the expected rate of inflation (to the nearest whole per cent)?

(f) Recalculate the machine's NPV if Flamingo Co. expected that:
   - the annual pre-tax machine running costs (£10,000 in the first year) would increase at a rate of 14 per cent p.a., and
   - the annual pre-tax revenue increases (£50,000 in the first year) would increase at a rate of 10 per cent p.a.

7. You have been asked to recommend which of the following freeze-drying units should be purchased by Bryers Laboratories Ltd. The HB1 unit is less expensive, but also less sturdy than the HB4 unit, and so is expected to have only half the useful life of the HB4. Summary information is as follows:

	Purchase price	*Annual running costs*	*Expected life*
HB1 unit	£ 6,000	£1,000	4 years
HB4 unit	£10,000	£1,100	8 years

The technical purchasing officer expects that each of these units will be replaceable at the end of its useful life for the same purchase price (in real terms). Bryers Laboratories Ltd. has a 10 per cent real opportunity cost of capital.

Recommend to the technical purchasing officer which freeze-dryer should be purchased (show your financial calculations).

8. Piper Co. has five potential CI projects, each one requiring progressive implementation over the next three years. The costs and expected NPVs of all five projects are shown below, together with capital rationing constraints in each of the next three years.

Project	*NPV (£000s)*	*Cash input required (£000s):* Year 1	Year 2	Year 3
1	45	10	6	15
2	70	15	15	18
3	42	8	5	19
4	55	5	20	4
5	60	15	12	18
Capital available for investment (£000s)		*Year 1* 44	*Year 2* 52	*Year 3* 60

(a) Formulate the objective function and constraint functions for this problem, for use in an integer linear programming model. (Assume that unused funds cannot be carried forward.)

(b) Using your integer LP formulation, solve the problem by computer. What is the best solution available to Piper Co? What will be the resulting total NPV?

(c) Now assume that projects 2 and 5 are mutually exclusive, and formulate a constraint function to reflect this. Add this constraint and re-solve the LP problem. What is your revised solution?

5

Determining the Required Rate of Return and Dealing with Risk

INTRODUCTION

An integral part of using discounted cash flow analyses to assess CI proposals is the determination of a required rate of return (RRR). In this chapter two different approaches to considering RRR are examined. The strengths and weaknesses of these two approaches are considered, and a "middle ground" approach is put forward as a practical response to the difficulties of RRR determination. Also, risk is considered as an important determinant of an appropriate RRR. Alternative approaches to considering risky projects are presented as useful decision support tools for CI analysis.

APPROACHES TO DETERMINING THE REQUIRED RATE OF RETURN

The RRR should reflect the "opportunity cost" of committing funds to a CI. This opportunity cost may be considered in two related ways:

- the cost of obtaining the funds for investment

- the return which could be expected on a similar type of investment (this return is forgone if the CI is undertaken).

These perspectives have different implicit assumptions, and lead to two approaches to determining a RRR for use in discounting the cashflows from CIs.

The "cost of funds" approach: weighted average cost of capital

The key to the cost of funds approach lies in determining the cost of the capital used to finance a CI. This is more complex than it might first appear. Where finance is raised specifically for a CI project, the cost of that finance (e.g. the interest rate on a bank loan) is known. However, organizations can rarely identify a CI with an individual source of financing. It is more realistic to view CIs as being financed from a "pool" of funds, derived from different sources at different times. So, the use of a "marginal" cost of capital (e.g. the cost of raising a specific loan) as the discount rate for a CI would be incorrect. It is more appropriate to calculate an *overall* cost of capital for a firm, which reflects the cost of the "pool" of organizational funds from which the CI is funded.

This "overall" cost is called the weighted average cost of capital (WACC). Determining the WACC has several steps:

- identifying the range of sources of long-term capital
- determining the cost of these capital sources
- determining their market value
- computing the WACC.

The main sources of long-term capital are debt, ordinary equity and preference shares. Note that short-term financing sources (e.g. creditors and overdrafts) are not included in the WACC, as they are not typically employed for the financing of long-term CIs.

The cost of these capital sources relates to the dividends payable on equity and the cost of interest for debt. The cost of debt is a function of the interest payable, the tax rate, any issuing expenses and the market value of the debt. Since interest paid on debt is an expense in the income statement, it is tax deductible (unlike dividends paid on equity). This is known as the "tax shield effect" of debt. Example 5.1 illustrates how this works.

EXAMPLE 5.1

The tax shield effect on the cost of debt

Lowe Co. can borrow at a rate of 16%. The Company is subject
to a tax rate of 35%. The after-tax cost of Lowe Co.'s debt can
be calculated as:

$$\text{After-tax debt cost} = \text{pre-tax debt cost} \times (1 - \text{tax rate})$$
$$= 16\% \times (1 - 0.35)$$
$$= \underline{10.4\%}$$

Debt capital is therefore generally cheaper than equity capital, due
to this tax break.[1]

The cost of equity capital sources (ordinary or preference shares)
for listed companies depends on dividend payable, the cost of
issuing equity and the market price of the shares. Retained earnings
are usually a less expensive source of equity capital than issuing
new shares, as retained earnings do not incur the transaction costs
associated with the public offering of shares. For smaller, unlisted
organizations, equity cost relates to opportunity cost – i.e. what
the equity capital could return if invested elsewhere.

However, for the purposes of this discussion it will simply be
assumed that the cost of these capital sources is known. Interested
readers can refer to other management accounting or finance texts
for the details of calculating the cost of debt, equity and preference
shares.

The weightings given to each source of funds in the WACC
calculation are based on the market value of the debt, ordinary
shares and preference shares (*not* their book values). The WACC
is therefore influenced by the relative proportions employed of
each capital source. However, it is assumed that organizations
operate at, or close to, their optimal mix of capital sources,
representing the lowest possible overall cost. To do otherwise
would be irrational, as most businesses will prefer a capital
structure which minimizes the cost of funds.

Once the sources of funds, their costs and their relative weighting

---

[1] Also, the use of after-tax capital costs is consistent with the use of after-tax
cashflows in the NPV analysis.

EXAMPLE 5.2

Calculating the weighted average cost of capital

Dean Co. has three sources of capital: debt, ordinary shares and preference shares. The costs of these capital sources have been calculated at 10%, 16% and 14% respectively. Dean Co. wants to know its weighted average cost of capital.

Finance source	Cost (%)	Market value (£000)	% of total capital	Weighted cost (%)
Debt	10	300	37.5	3.75
Ordinary shares	16	400	50.0	8.00
Preference shares	14	100	12.5	1.75
		800	100.0	13.50

So, Dean Co. has a WACC of 13.5%.

in the capital structure have been determined, it is a simple task to compute the WACC. Example 5.2 illustrates a simple WACC calculation.

There are, however, two problems with using the WACC as an RRR for *all* CI projects. The WACC reflects the current cost of a pool of funds used for financing the current investments of the organization. If a CI project is outside the normal activity or business area, then it may have a different risk profile to that of normal investments. In this case, the WACC is no longer an appropriate RRR, as it does not adequately take account of the different risk of the CI being assessed.

The second problem arises where the CI project is sufficiently large to affect the financing structure. The WACC approach assumes that the relative weightings of the capital sources remains the same after a new CI is financed. If, for example, a substantial loan had to be raised to finance a CI, this assumption may no longer hold true, and the WACC will change.

Although the WACC approach offers a simple approach to determining an RRR, it has clear weaknesses. It is often unrealistic to assume that all CI projects have the same risk and that this riskiness corresponds to the organization's "normal" investments. Therefore, as it takes no account of risk, the use of WACC is not a theoretically correct approach to determining the RRR.

The "risk–adjusted return" approach: CAPM

Modern portfolio theory from the economics and finance literature has provided an approach to determining project RRRs which *does* take risk into account. The risk–return relationship is illustrated in the securities market line (SML), as shown in Figure 5.1. The SML illustrates that a higher risk project has a correspondingly higher RRR. A "risk-free" investment[2] carries a basic "risk-free rate of return", and all investments with higher risk carry an RRR premium. This general approach has become known as the "capital asset pricing model" (CAPM) approach to determining appropriate required rates of return for risky investments.

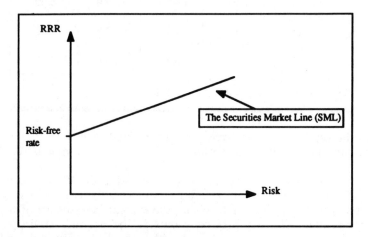

Figure 5.1 The risk–return relationship

Compare this approach to the WACC method where *all* projects are discounted at the WACC. Figure 5.2 illustrates the placement of four CI projects in relation to these two RRR determination approaches. In Figure 5.2, projects A and B offer the same rates of return, but have differing risk profiles. The same is true for projects C and D. Using the WACC approach, A and B would

---

[2] Government securities, for example, are generally considered to be "risk-free investments".

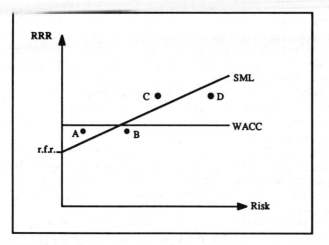

Figure 5.2 Weighted average cost of capital (WACC) v. securities
market line (SML)

both be rejected as they return less than the WACC. Projects C
and D would be accepted as their returns exceed the organization's
WACC.

However, when the riskiness of these projects is considered, B
and D both offer returns *less* than what would be required to
compensate for their riskiness (i.e. they are below the SML).
Projects A and C are both above the SML and should be accepted.

It is clear that the WACC, by not accounting for risk, can lead
to the incorrect acceptance of high return (but overly high risk)
projects, and the incorrect rejection of low return (but low risk)
projects. Using the SML leads to the correct risk-adjusted
accept/reject decisions.

Using the SML has two practical difficulties:

1. How is the "riskiness" of a project determined (i.e. where is
    it on the SML x-axis)?
2. What RRR is appropriate for the level of risk (i.e. where is
    it on the SML y-axis)?

Measuring risk

"Risk" can be defined as the volatility of returns from an
investment. All investments can expect some volatility, simply as
a result of changes in the overall economy or market. However,
some investments are more volatile than others.

A measure of risk developed from portfolio theory is beta (β). Beta is an expression of the "market sensitivity" of an investment, or how volatile it is compared with the "normal" volatility of the market. A beta of 1 indicates that changes in an investment's returns correspond exactly to overall market fluctuations. A beta of less than 1 reflects a low-risk project whose returns are more stable than the overall market, and a beta of greater than 1 indicates an investment whose returns are more volatile than can be expected from overall market movements.

Although beta provides a measure of risk, it is difficult in practice to find the exact beta of a particular CI project. Betas are normally determined from sharemarket information, where the movement in a *company*'s returns (reflected by share price) can be observed.

If a publicly-listed company is considering a CI project which is "typical" of its usual business operations, then the company's overall market riskiness (as measured by beta) can provide an indication of the risk of the project. However, firms often have most difficulty in arriving at appropriate risk measures for projects which are outside their normal area of activity. In this case, it may be possible to estimate project betas by using as surrogates the market betas of companies who operate in areas of activity similar to that proposed in the CI project.

For example, if a firm which normally manufactures furniture proposes to expand into a furniture retailing investment, new and different risks may be expected. Therefore, it would be more appropriate to consider the betas of other companies which are currently in the furniture retailing business, than to rely on the firm's own current market beta.

There are, however, two problems with using sharemarket betas as surrogates for project betas. First, sharemarkets measure the value of returns on *equity* (i.e. to the shareholder), not the return on assets (i.e. on the company's investments). The equity beta reflects both the asset beta (the surrogate for the CI project) and riskiness due to the company's financing structure. Shareholders will perceive a company as more risky if its debt-to-equity ratio is higher, and this is reflected in market betas.

Financing structure is irrelevant to the riskiness of the type of business. For example, an investment in a fast-food sales development has an inherent business risk which is the same no matter whether the project is undertaken by a highly or lowly geared business. So, to find the asset beta we must "ungear" the sharemarket beta to remove this financial structure risk effect.

Ungearing market betas is problematic. Taking a basic approach we can work from the relationship that:

$$\beta \text{ asset} = (\beta \text{ debt} \times \frac{D}{D+E}) + (\beta \text{ equity} \times \frac{E}{D+E})$$

Where: D = market value of debt

E = market value of equity

β asset = the "business risk" to be used in finding an RRR surrogate

β debt = the riskiness of the company's debt borrowings, and

β equity = the sharemarket beta, relating to equity returns.

Often, the simplifying assumption is made that β debt = zero, i.e. the company can borrow at the risk-free rate. This assumption is not always realistic, but will be used here to illustrate a simple approach to finding the ungeared asset beta.

EXAMPLE 5.3

Finding the asset beta

Koorey Co. has a market beta (β equity) of 1.6. We wish to find its β assets as a surrogate for the riskiness of a CI we are appraising, which is in the normal line of business of Koorey Co. We know that Koorey Co. has a 30% debt ratio (assume β debt = 0).

$$\beta \text{ asset} = (\beta \text{ debt} \times \frac{D}{D+E}) + (\beta \text{ equity} \times \frac{E}{D+E})$$
$$= 0 + [1.6 \times (1-0.30)]$$
$$= 1.6 \times 0.70$$
$$= \underline{1.12}$$

Hence, the β asset of 1.12 provides a measure of the business risk of the activities of Koorey Co.

Alternatively, where possible it is preferable to use an average of the β assets of several companies. The ability to do this depends on the availability of market betas and financial structure information on a number of companies in a closely related business area.

The second problem with using company betas as surrogates for project betas arises because there is a difference between the risk characteristics of a portfolio of investments (e.g. a company) and a single investment (e.g. the CI to be evaluated). If the company (or group of companies) used as a risk surrogate has a diversified range of investments, then its inherent riskiness may be lower as a result of this diversification. This diversified asset beta is then not appropriate for use as a surrogate for a single project beta.

However, if we are able to identify a relatively undiversified company, whose business activity is similar to that of the CI project we aim to assess, then a company asset beta can be useful. This is not always easy in practice, and is a difficulty inherent in the CAPM approach to determining required rates of return.

Also, the riskiness of any single project may differ from its risk impact on an organization once it becomes part of that organization's portfolio of investments. As part of a portfolio, the riskiness of a project is determined by its covariance with other projects in that portfolio. In effect, an organization diversifies its portfolio by adding a project which has different risk characteristics to the other investments held. This group of investments, all responding to market changes in different ways, can act as "buffers" for each other's risk. So, from the organization's point of view, overall risk can be reduced by combining investment projects of differing types and individual risk characteristics.

Here though, there is an argument that diversification at the organizational level is irrelevant to the goal of maximizing shareholder wealth. Shareholders are able to diversify for themselves, by holding shares in a range of business areas. There is, theoretically, no need for organizations to seek diversification on behalf of their shareholders. This view would suggest that the portfolio effects of an individual CI project are unimportant in assessing the RRR for that individual project. The CI decision-maker should not place value on the project's ability (or inability) to lessen the organization's portfolio risk, as the owners, theoretically, place no value on diversification of an individual organization's investments.

Theoretically, the shareholder is concerned only with a CI project's ability to compensate for its own project risk (β), so an acceptable project must be above (or at least on) the securities market line. A CI decision-maker who is acting to maximize shareholders' wealth should therefore only be concerned with a project's own risk and return, irrespective of the project's relationship to other investments currently held by the organization.

So, although there are practical difficulties with using beta as a measure of risk, it provides a useful indication of what the "risk" of a CI project is. As noted, this approach is especially useful when considering a CI which is outside the normal area of business activity. Here, consideration of beta measures for other firms in the appropriate industry can help the CI decision-maker to avoid mistakes where the riskiness of a CI project is incorrectly estimated. Note the use of the word "estimated". It would be rash to suggest that this (or any other) relatively simple approach can produce a definitive project risk measure. What it offers is an educated estimate.

Using beta as a surrogate for the riskiness of the type of business involved in our CI project, we can now find an appropriate RRR at which to discount the cashflows from the CI to find its NPV.

What is the appropriate required rate of return?

The beta risk measure is used in conjunction with the capital asset pricing model (CAPM), which expresses a relationship between an investment's riskiness and its RRR. The CAPM risk–return relationship is expressed below.

The CAPM risk–return relationship

$$RRR_A = R_f + [(R_m - R_f) \times \beta_A]$$

Where: RRR_A = the required rate of return on the asset/investment in question
R_f = the risk free rate of return
R_m = the market return
β_A = the beta of the asset/investment in question.

The term $(R_m - R_f)$ reflects the "market premium", that is, the return over and above the risk-free rate which the market earns. So if a CI was of average market risk (beta = 1) then it could be expected to earn this same premium.

Example 5.4 shows the calculation of an appropriate RRR using the CAPM approach as applied to the investment with a beta of 1.12 from Example 5.3.

EXAMPLE 5.4

Using the CAPM to determine the required rate of return

$$\text{Assume: } R_f = 10\%$$
$$R_m = 18\%$$

$$RRR_A = R_f + [(R_m - R_f) \times \beta_A]$$
$$= 10\% + (18\% - 10\%) \times 1.12$$
$$= 10\% + 8.96\%$$
$$= \underline{18.96\%}$$

So, the riskiness of this investment (greater than that of the overall market) suggests that it should earn a RRR of about 19% (greater than the market return).

In Example 5.4, the 19 per cent RRR could then be used as the discount rate in determining the NPV of a CI project in the same business area as Koorey Co. (from Example 5.3).

The CAPM approach to determining the RRR is complex. There are many implicit assumptions, both in the CAPM model itself and in its application. Some of these assumptions include:

- that the market is efficient and market betas are reliable
- that a single time period model (the CAPM) can be appropriately transferred to the assessment of multiple time period CIs[3]
- that the beta of debt is zero, or can be found
- that capital markets are perfect (e.g. no taxes or information costs) and investors are economically rational and risk averse.

Yet, despite its imperfections[4] and practical difficulties, the CAPM approach is the most theoretically correct way to determine risk-adjusted RRRs. However, where a CI project is close to an organization's "normal" type of investment, a more simple approach may be useful. This approach is based on the SML relationship and goes some way towards addressing the risk concern.

---

[3] In theory, adjustments must be made to the CAPM model to allow for this problem. These adjustments are complex and beyond the scope of this book. Suffice to say, the time perspective problem either adds to the complexity of using the CAPM approach, or detracts from the reliability of its results.

[4] Theoretical difficulties have been noted in the CAPM; see for example Roll (1977) in the list of further readings.

A pragmatic approach: adjusted required rates of return

An organization may use its WACC as an indication of its "normal" RRR on a project of "average" business risk. Then, subjective adjustments to RRR can be made for those CIs whose risk characteristics are outside the "normal" type of investment.

For example, a firm with a known WACC may improve upon the blanket application of this WACC by devising three risk categories: low risk, average risk and high risk. Example 5.5 illustrates this approach.

EXAMPLE 5.5

Subjective risk-class adjustment to the WACC

Currently, the risk-free rate is 10% and Tully Co. has determined its WACC to be 18%. CI analysts at Tully Co. decide to use the following risk categories for assessing CI projects:

- low risk (RRR = 14%)
- average risk (RRR = 18%) and
- high risk (RRR = 24%).

This categorization can be shown to approximate an SML approach:

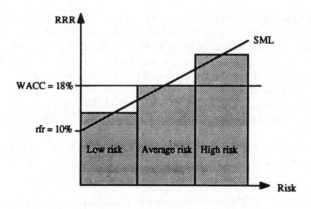

While not theoretically correct, this approach has three advantages over the single WACC approach:[5]

1. It can lessen the chances of incorrect decisions, as it partially accounts for risk.
2. It forces CI decision-makers to explicitly consider riskiness of CI projects.
3   It forces CI decision-makers to explicitly consider appropriate RRRs and may therefore encourage increased use of market information.

Required rate of return determination: summary

Two basic approaches to determining the RRR for use in NPV analyses have been explored. The WACC approach gives an appreciation of the cost of the "pool" of capital employed by an organization. WACC may be regarded as a guideline to RRR where a CI project is within the "normal investment activity" of an organization, and where it will not, in itself, require any change to the organization's capital structure. However, the WACC approach is not appropriate for use with CI projects of significantly different risk profiles.

The CAPM (SML) approach provides a theoretically correct, comprehensive approach to risk-adjusted RRR determination. However, the model's assumptions have been criticized as unrealistic, and it is complex to use and relies on the availability and accuracy of much information which is external to the organization.

A simplified approach using "risk classes" and adjusted WACC-required rates of return is put forward as a pragmatic, though subjective, approach to at least partially addressing the risk issue. Part of the strength of this approach lies in its requirement for CI decision-makers to at least explicitly consider risk and the RRR, rather than mechanically applying a single RRR to all CIs. Also, given the inherent uncertainty in many of the inputs to the NPV analysis, complex consideration of an "accurate" RRR may be less important.

Where a CI represents an activity which is outside the organization's normal investment experience, the RRR issue

---

[5] Sundem (1974, p. 320) noted that "there is a possibility to increase greatly the performance of a net present value model by assigning projects to two or three risk classes and using a different discount rate for evaluating projects in each risk class".

becomes difficult. In this situation, the CAPM approach, by learning from the market, holds the key to gaining an improved perspective on an appropriate RRR.

ALTERNATIVE APPROACHES TO ASSESSING RISKY CAPITAL INVESTMENTS

So far, it has been shown that the riskiness of CI projects can be dealt with using a risk-adjusted discount rate or required rate of return. However, there are alternative approaches to assessing risky CIs, the more sophisticated of which come primarily from the operations research (OR) literature. In this next section the following approaches to assessing risky CIs are considered:

- the assignment of outcome probabilities
- simulation
- sensitivity analysis
- game theory.

Assigning outcome probabilities

The use of probabilities assigned to a range of possible outcomes is a simple approach to assessing risky CIs. This approach requires that the CI decision-maker can foresee the range of possible outcomes and can estimate the probability of each of these outcomes occurring. A typical categorization of outcomes might be "pessimistic", "most likely" and "optimistic", reflecting a risky situation where a down-side and up-side to CI returns exist. Example 5.6 illustrates this approach.

EXAMPLE 5.6

Assessing a risky CI project using probability assignments

Grant Co. is considering investing in Project X, which has an expected NPV of +£15,000. The CI controller at Grant Co. is concerned about the riskiness of Project X and, rather than accepting it based on its expected positive NPV, investigates the likelihood of other outcomes. She determines the following:

Outcome	Probability	NPV	Weighted NPV
Optimistic	10%	+£22,000	+£2,200
Most likely	50%	+£15,000	+£7,500
Pessimistic	40%	−£28,000	−£11,200
Weighted average NPV =			−£1,500

So, even though +£15,000 is the "most likely" outcome, the high probability of a much worse result means that the *expected* NPV (based on probability assignations) is negative, and the project should be rejected.

Example 5.6 illustrates the danger of ignoring risk (the "spread" of possible returns) in a CI project. The "expected value" of a CI may be quite different from its "most likely" value; reliance on "most likely" results can lead to incorrect decisions.

The answer, though, does not lie with expected NPVs alone. The spread of results is equally important in considering the attractiveness of a CI. Example 5.7 illustrates how two CIs can have identical expected NPVs, but quite different risk characteristics.

EXAMPLE 5.7

Expected NPV and the spread of possible outcomes

Projects C and D both have expected NPVs of £50,000. However, once the range of possible outcomes is considered, it is clear that the two projects have differing risk profiles.

Project C	
NPV Outcome	*Probability*
£20,000	5%
£30,000	10%
£40,000	20%
£50,000	30%
£60,000	20%
£70,000	10%
£80,000	5%

Project D	
NPV Outcome	*Probability*
£45,000	10%
£50,000	80%
£55,000	10%

Project C has a much wider distribution of possible outcomes, and so is more risky than Project D. This would not be reflected by considering their expected NPVs alone.

The choice between investments C and D depends on the risk preferences of the investor. It is assumed (in economic theory) that investors are risk averse, and so Project D would normally be preferred as it provides the same expected return as Project C, but at a lower risk level.

The weakness of the probability assignment approach is its subjectivity. Differing assessments of possible outcomes and their probabilities can lead to totally different expected NPVs. But, as an improvement on single-outcome assessment, using probability distributions of possible outcomes is a simple way of ensuring that risk is not ignored.

Simulation

Simulation techniques are an extension of the probability approach outlined above. The probability approach involves estimating only one outcome – the CI's return or NPV. For most CI projects, a number of factors influence this final result, including projected costs, projected revenues, the required rate of return, the life of the investment and its expected salvage value. Simulation allows for each of these inputs to be treated as risky.[6]

Using a simulation approach (sometimes called "Monte Carlo simulation"), a CI decision-maker must:

---

[6] Hertz (1964) provides an excellent early discussion of the simulation approach.

1. identify the key variables of the CI project
2. consider the range of values which these variables might assume
3. assign probabilities to each of these possible values
4. (usually) set up a computer application to conduct the simulation.

The computer simulation randomly selects a value for each of the key variables, based on the possible outcomes and probabilities identified by the decision-maker. Using these values, the computer then computes the NPV of the CI project. After a large number of iterations, an "expected" NPV emerges, together with the range of possible NPV outcomes which gives the decision-maker a sense of the riskiness associated with the CI. The output of a simulation exercise has great intuitive appeal, providing useful results which are easily understood.

Small-scale simulation can, of course, be conducted without the aid of a computer. However, the utility of the simulation technique depends on the complexity of the inputs to the CI decision and the number of iterations which are performed, so non-computerized simulation is rarely useful.

When using simulation, care must be taken to allow for dependence between variables (for example, there might be an association between the life of a project and its expected salvage value). The success of simulation ultimately depends on the decision-maker, who must ensure that all key variables have been identified and that the range of values and probabilities attached to these outcomes are realistic.

Sensitivity analysis

Sensitivity analysis is similar to simulation, but is less comprehensive and complex. Using this approach, those inputs to the CI decision which have a *significant* impact on the ultimate CI outcome are identified. This is achieved by recalculating the NPV of a project, changing only one key variable at a time so that its effect on the CI outcome can be determined.

If a change in the value of a key variable has little effect on the NPV outcome, then a correct investment decision is unlikely to rest on the accuracy of that variable's estimated value. However, where a small change in the value of a variable produces a significant impact on the CI's viability, the CI is said to be highly "sensitive" to that variable, as the variable is making a significant contribution to the project's riskiness. In that case, the decision-maker is alerted to the need for accuracy in determining the likely value of that estimate, and further investigation of that variable may be warranted. Where a variable is found to be crucial to the outcome of a CI, and that variable is inherently risky (or uncertain), this may influence the decision to invest in a marginal CI. Therefore, the value of sensitivity analysis is twofold:

1. It allows identification of variables which significantly impact on the CI's outcome, so that their correct estimation may be fully considered.
2. It assists in identifying CIs which are highly risky due to the volatile (or uncertain) nature of key variables, and allows for the calculation of an "expected" NPV for these projects.

Sensitivity analysis is also useful as a precursor to simulation, so that the decision-maker can focus upon gaining accurate estimation data for those variables which are crucial to the CI's outcome.

One difficulty in the use of sensitivity analysis arises where key variables are mutually dependent. This effect is best dealt with using simulation, although it can be partially overcome by treating dependent variables as a single variable and adjusting their values proportionately, based on their expected relationship.

Game theory

Game theory is useful where probability estimates cannot easily be arrived at. Simple game theory takes a conservative approach, aiming to minimize the loss or "regret" from making a bad CI decision. Therefore, this approach may not produce the "best" investment decision, but offers ways of eliminating what may be perceived as the most risky options.

One game theory approach to selecting between uncertain CI projects is known as the "minimax" approach. This approach helps the CI decision-maker to select the best of the worst possible outcomes which may eventuate – i.e. it protects against a very bad outcome. Another similar method is called the "minimax regret" approach, which focuses upon the opportunity cost of making an incorrect decision, and lessens the chances of the CI decision-maker looking bad after the event (an appealing approach for many CI decision-makers!).

Example 5.8 illustrates the minimax and minimax regret procedures, as applied to a choice between two uncertain CI options.

EXAMPLE 5.8

Game theory: the minimax and minimax regret approaches

Roberts Co. has a choice of investing in two production plants, one large and one small. If market demand for their product is high, the larger plant is expected to have the higher NPV. But if demand is low, high fixed costs for the larger plant mean that the smaller plant then has the higher NPV. Unfortunately, Roberts Co. has no information on the likelihood of these market demand scenarios occurring. The options, possible market demands and expected NPV results are shown below.

Plant size

		small	large
Level of	*high*	NPV = +£100,000	NPV = +£180,000
demand	*low*	NPV = +£80,000	NPV = +£40,000

Using the minimax approach, Roberts Co. would identify the worst possible (minimum) outcomes under each market scenario, i.e. (high demand–small plant; NPV = £100,000) and (low demand–large plant; NPV = £40,000). They would then select the investment option which gives the best (maximum) of these results, i.e. (high demand–small plant). So, the small plant option would be selected.

Using the minimax regret approach, Roberts Co. would calculate the "opportunity cost" (OC) or "regret" of making an incorrect decision under each market scenario. For example, selecting the small plant option when demand is high produces an NPV of only £100,000, which is £80,000 less than the NPV which could have been produced by selecting a large plant. Therefore, choosing the small plant has an opportunity cost of £80,000. Selecting the large plant when demand is high has a zero opportunity cost — it is the best possible option. The opportunity cost table is

Plant size

		small	large
Level of	*high*	O.C. = £80,000	O.C. = 0
demand	*low*	O.C. = 0	O.C. = £40,000

So the potential "regret" for each plant size option is £80,000 for the small plant and £40,000 for the large plant. Using this approach, the large plant would be preferred as it has the lower potential "regret".

In Example 5.8, the minimax and minimax regret approaches have produced conflicting CI project selections. This is not uncommon, and is a problem of this approach.

However, where probability distributions cannot be ascertained for possible outcomes, game theory offers an alternative approach to eliminating the "worst choice" decisions, providing a "safety net" for the CI decision-maker.

Analysing risky CIs using OR methods: summary

Some of the techniques adopted in the CI analysis literature from operations research (OR) are complex to use and may be intuitively difficult to interpret. Other methods (such as game theory) are simplistic, and the reliability of their outputs suffers as a result. However, where the use of a risk-adjusted discount rate does not adequately capture the riskiness or uncertainty inherent in a CI proposal, these OR techniques represent additional decision-support tools for the decision-maker.

SUMMARY

In this chapter the issues of risk and determining the required rate of return were considered. Two approaches to determining the RRR (weighted average cost of capital and the CAPM approach) were outlined and compared. It was shown that WACC can be useful where the CI project being assessed is in the normal line of business of the organization, but may be misleading where the project has an atypical risk profile. The CAPM approach takes better account of individual project riskiness, but can be difficult to use in practice. As a pragmatic solution, it was proposed that "risk classes" can be useful in at least partially accounting for differing inherent riskiness in individual CI projects.

There are a number of supplementary decision-support tools (mainly derived from the OR literature) which can add depth to a consideration of the range of CI results which might occur. Examples of these OR approaches were outlined and demonstrated in this chapter. Consideration of risk using these techniques can help the decision-maker to pinpoint, and note the implications of, those factors which are not known. Grappling with what is unknown is often just as important as assessing those things which are known!

In the next chapter we take a look at the research evidence for how CI decision-making occurs in practice. Learning from these empirical observations, we may be in a better position to reflect on the nexus between theory and practice and its implications for improved CI decision-making.

Suggestions for further reading

Carroll, J.J. and Newbould, G.D. (1987). "Spreadsheets simplify sensitivity analysis for capital decisions", *Healthcare Financial Management*, Vol. 41 (6), June, pp. 78–88.

Clarke, P. and Paquette, L. (1988). "Financial management with Lotus 1-2-3", *Accountancy (UK)*, Vol. 102 (1144), December, pp. 132–3.

Gapenski, L.C. (1990). "Using Monte Carlo simulation to make better capital investment decisions", *Hospital and Health Care Services Administration*, Vol. 35 (2), Summer, pp. 207–19.

Hertz, D.B. (1964). "Risk analysis in capital investment", *Harvard Business Review*, January/February, pp. 175–86.

Ho, S.S.M. and Pike, R.H. (1991). "Risk analysis in capital budgeting contexts: Simple or sophisticated?" *Accounting and Business Research*, Vol. 21 (83), pp. 227–38.

Hull, J.C. (1980). *The Evaluation of Risk in Business Investment*, Pergamon Press, Oxford.

Roll, R. (1977). "A critique of the asset pricing theory's tests; Part 1: On past and potential testability of the theory", *Journal of Financial Economics*, Vol. 4, March, pp. 129–76.

Sundem, G.L. (1974). "Evaluating simplified capital budgeting models using a time–state preference metric", *The Accounting Review*, Vol. 49 (2), April, pp. 306–20.

Wiseman, A. (1988). "Operational research: A toolkit for effective decision-making", *Management Accounting (UK)*, Vol. 66 (11), December, p. 36.

Problems

1. What is "risk"? How might the riskiness of a CI project be measured?
2. Discuss the differences between the "weighted average cost of capital" and the "capital asset pricing model" approaches to determining a CI's required rate of return.
3. What are the practical difficulties of using the CAPM approach to finding the risk-adjusted required rate of return for a CI project?
4. A machine which your organization is considering purchasing has the following relevant information:
   - initial purchase price = £150,000
   - expected life = eight years
   - expected salvage value = £20,000
   - annual pre-tax running costs = £15,000
   - annual pre-tax revenue increase due to the machine's efficiency = £60,000
   - required increase in raw materials inventory = £15,000 (to be liquidated at the end of the asset's life for £15,000)
   - allowable asset writing down allowance = 25% p.a. on diminishing value
   - tax rate = 35%
   - after-tax real required rate of return = 10%; after-tax nominal required rate of return = 18%
   - it is near the end of your organization's financial year.

Required:
(a) Using the real expected cashflows given above, calculate the NPV of the decision to purchase the new machine.
(b) Using a Lotus 1-2-3 (or equivalent) spreadsheet, set up cells representing the cashflows associated with the machine purchase. Be sure to include:
   (i) provision for the automatic calculation of the amount (and timing) of the taxation effects from these running costs and revenues
   (ii) a general cell formula for the calculation of taxation effects from the asset's writing down allowances.
   You can then use the NPV function within Lotus 1-2-3 to calculate the NPV of the cashflows at any selected required rate of return.
(c) Using your spreadsheet, determine the relative sensitivity of the NPV result to changes in the following variables:
   (i) the expected life of the asset

      (ii) the asset's salvage value
      (iii) the expected annual running costs
      (iv) the expected annual revenues
      (v) the required rate of return.
      (Hint: try changing these variables by known percentages and then observing the percentage change created in the NPV result.)

    (d) Which variables in the machine purchase decision (if any) do you think warrant further investigation, based on your sensitivity analyses?

5. You wish to estimate a risk-adjusted RRR for use in assessing a furniture manufacturing business. You have gathered information on a publicly listed company (Decor Co.) which is in the sole business of manufacturing furniture, and which you consider provides a good guideline for the business you wish to assess. Your information on Decor Co. is as follows:

- the company is financed in the ratio of 40% debt and 60% equity
- Decor Co. is a stable company which can borrow at the risk-free rate
- the company's sharemarket beta is 1.8.

What required rate of return does this suggest, for use in your analysis of the furniture manufacturing business?

6. Shelford Co. wants to find an appropriate required rate of return (RRR) for use in calculating the NPV of a proposed capital investment in the manufacture of sporting equipment. You have the following information:

- Shelford Co. has two sources of long-term capital:
  - (i) a long-term loan at 20% interest, with a market value of £40,000
  - (ii) ordinary shares at a cost (due to dividends paid) of 15%, with a market value of £60,000.
- Shelford Co.'s tax rate is 30%.
- The risk-free rate is currently 4%.
- The share market premium is currently 9% above the risk-free rate.
- The market beta (β) for a well-known sporting goods manufacturing company is currently 1.9. This company has a debt-to-equity ratio of 20:80, and can borrow at the risk-free rate.

Required:

(a) Calculate the weighted average cost of capital for Shelford Co.

(b) Calculate a market-based RRR which you consider would

be appropriate for use in assessing the sporting equipment manufacturing CI proposal.

(c) What can you infer about the likely "riskiness" of Shelford Co.'s normal investment activities, compared with this new CI proposal? Justify your answer.

7. The CI director of Heslop Co. has to decide between two mutually exclusive CI projects. The director estimates that there are three possible NPV outcomes for each of these projects, depending on the prevailing economic conditions over the next few years. However, he has no information on the probabilities of these possible economic conditions. Therefore, his main concern is to eliminate the project option which would make him look *worst* if things turned out badly. The director has summarized his various NPV estimates as follows:

Project

		Option 1	*Option 2*
Economic conditions	*poor*	NPV = −£200,000	NPV = −£160,000
	average	NPV = +£120,000	NPV = +£100,000
	excellent	NPV = +£400,000	NPV = +£260,000

Required:

(a) (i)   Given the CI director's objective of minimizing the chances of looking bad if things do not go well, what approach should be taken to assessing the two mutually exclusive projects?

(ii) Using the approach you identified in (i), show how the CI director could decide between the two projects so as to best achieve his objective.

(b) Assume now that you have contacted an economic analyst who predicts the following probability distribution of economic outcomes:

poor − 20%
average − 50%
excellent − 30%

Which project would you now recommend be accepted? Show supporting calculations.

(c) Discuss any differences between your results in (a) and (b) above.

6

What Do We Know About Capital Investment Practice?

INTRODUCTION

The literature documenting research into capital budgeting practice spans more than three decades. It reveals a predominant approach to discovering capital budgeting practice by surveying using questionnaire research instruments. The findings of such surveys have been the basis of inferences and conclusions by many research authors, conclusions which have become widely accepted as representing extant knowledge of capital budgeting practice. Writings which represent major, or unique contributions to the literature will form the focus of the review presented in this chapter. Therefore, while not exhaustive, this chapter represents a comprehensive examination of the empirical CI research literature.

The authors of much of this literature appear to share the common conception of CI as a "process", as outlined in Chapter 2. Therefore, their research findings can be considered under headings derived from Figure 2.1, p. 10:

1. identification of potential investments
2. analysis and acceptance

3. post audit
4. formal CI systems
5. organizational personnel
6. strategic planning.

THE IDENTIFICATION OF POTENTIAL INVESTMENTS

As noted earlier, King (1975, p. 73) identified what he called the "triggering" phase of CI, and noted that CI theory failed to recognize that "in practice each opportunity for investment must be identified and exploited".

Klammer (1972) was one of the few authors to consider idea generation, finding that 82 per cent of respondents actively sought investment ideas in 1959, with this figure rising to 94 per cent in 1970. However, Klammer's results contrast strongly with those of much other research, as noted by Mukherjee and Henderson (1987, p. 80). These authors noted in particular that Klammer's observations were at odds with those of Istvan (1961a) who found that ". . . only one of the 48 firms [he] interviewed made any special effort to stimulate capital investment".

More recent work continues to produce mixed evidence of the search for investment ideas. Pike (1983b, p. 204) found that 83 per cent of his UK survey respondents conducted specific search procedures, stimulated by difficulty in generating enough profitable investments. However, McIntyre and Coulthurst (1987, p. 39) found a lack of organized searching for investment ideas, with only 49 per cent of their UK respondents claiming to do so. They suggest a possible explanation for these apparent contradictions, noting that the incidence of investment searching may increase the larger the organization.

Whatever the reasons, there is still no clear indication of the nature or extent of CI idea generation in practice, and little attention has been given to the nature of the stimuli which trigger searches for investment opportunities.

There is also little agreement on the organizational levels from which investment ideas arise. Mukherjee and Henderson (1987, p. 80) assert that "new project ideas come from lower levels in the managerial organisation", citing the works of Istvan (1961b), Mao (1970) and Petty, Scott and Bird (1975) in support of this conclusion. Yet, in their survey of medium-sized businesses, McIntyre and Coulthurst (1987, p. 39) noted that all types of investment ideas were "found to predominate from top management of the companies, indicating a rather more limited source than found in surveys of larger companies".

While Petty, Scott and Bird (1975, p. 162) observed that lower organizational levels *collectively* account for more investment proposals than do higher levels, they also noted that "no *single* level in the organizational hierarchy dominates the inception of investment proposals". So here again, the evidence is mixed.

It also seems that not all types of CI ideas are encouraged. Scapens and Sale (1981, p. 406) noted that most of their UK and USA respondents controlled the types of proposals received via the capital expenditure budget, using broad guidelines from company headquarters as to what constituted acceptable proposals. The apparent aim is to ensure that projects proposed are in line with group objectives, yet "guidelines" potentially act as a limiting factor on the generation of capital expenditure ideas.

From the limited research evidence a picture emerges of a controlled "inspiration" process. Acceptable projects are closely defined, and the only noted stimulus for active searches is a felt lack of profitable investments. It also appears that investment proposals emanate from lower hierarchical levels in larger firms, with only those proposals requiring a change of policy or product attracting the attention of corporate level decision-makers. In smaller firms, where the hierarchy may be less pronounced, there is more evidence of high-level leadership in project generation.

FORMAL STRUCTURES

When surveyed, respondents can only proffer a particular view of how CI is undertaken in their organizations, often reflecting formal CI structures which may not equate to actual practice. Nevertheless formal procedures are a significant influence on practice, and are considered in the research literature.

Standardized documentation of procedures was an early manifestation of formal CI structures noted in the survey literature. Klammer (1972) found that the use of standard forms had been consistently high over the period 1959 to 1970, growing from 84 per cent to 97 per cent. UK surveys produced similar results. McIntyre and Coulthurst (1987, p. 39) found that 58 per cent of medium-sized UK companies had written CI procedures, while 59 per cent had standardized CI documentation. Pike (1988, p. 344) noted that the use of CI manuals in large UK firms had increased by 19 per cent since 1975, up to 84 per cent. In Australia, Lilleyman's 1984 survey revealed only 72 per cent of respondents using standard forms and 53 per cent having a CI manual. So apparently, while the use of standardized documentation and procedures has seemed relatively widespread, there are inconsistent results in the literature.

Central management (or review) committees have been noted as a formal organizational structure created to deal with CI. In 1975 Gitman and Forrester found that 75 per cent of US manufacturing firms surveyed used "central review committees" for approving CI proposals. Pike (1983b) found higher usage of review committees in the UK (85 per cent), while Lilleyman's (1984) Australian results were considerably lower, at 49 per cent. Again, there is little consensus in the literature.

The links between organizational hierarchy and CI have been explored by several authors. Petty, Scott and Bird (1975, p. 170) found that the authority for CI decisions in large US firms often rested with the board of directors, an executive committee, the CEO or some operating committee. Yet, Scapens and Sale (1981, p. 402) noted the delegation of much of this authority, with spending limits assigned to different hierarchical levels.

The literature suggests that much of the analysis and decision-making in CI is conducted at lower organizational levels, although the responsibility often rests with top management. Ross (1986) observed in his case study research that a typical CI approved hierarchy would see a project go first to a plant manager (or equivalent), then be evaluated by a corporate engineer and sent to divisional headquarters as part of a *group* of requests. This aggregation of capital projects as they proceed up the hierarchy indicates that much of the real responsibility for approval rests at the lower organizational levels, whilst higher-level approval tends to be a "rubber stamping" of lower-level decisions. Marsh *et al.* (1988, p. 23) made an observation along these lines, noting a UK case where a "group CEO sat on the divisional board [and] the division referred to the group's approval as 'rubber stamping'."

Baxter and Hirst (1986) cast doubt on the usefulness of formal CI information systems and processes in their case study of a CI decision in an Australian firm. They found (p. 21) that "the decision is best described by artifactual and political models of choice" and "information was used in a manner consistent with . . . 'ammunition' and 'rationalisation' analogies". Baxter and Hirst noted (p. 24) that the information used "did not emanate from the organisation's formal accounting system but was generated . . . to satisfy the imperatives of the decision process".

They concluded that the formal organizational information system failed to provide information that was relevant.

This indicates that the "procedures" of CI practice require further exploration. Baxter and Hirst (p. 22) found an example of "non-rational" CI decision-making, a perspective which brings into question the underlying premises of CI theory as a rational, wealth-maximizing activity.

ANALYSIS AND ACCEPTANCE

The analysis and acceptance of CI proposals can be divided into four issues:

1. the use of the analysis techniques (i.e. PP, AROR, NPV, IRR and PI)
2. the influence of non-financial factors on CI evaluation
3. the determination of cashflow data and the required rate of return (RRR)
4. risk analysis and the use of operations research (OR) tools.

Use of analysis techniques

Users of more common, and perhaps intuitively easier, tools such as PP and AROR have been increasingly castigated for failing to make "correct" assessments of project value. Even for those who use DCF techniques, the IRR versus NPV debate is not settled, although the weight of academic opinion appears to favour NPV (see, for example, the discussion provided by Horngren and Foster, 1991, p. 722). Much of the investigation of CI practice has concentrated on the extent to which DCF methods have been adopted in practice.

One of the earliest attempts to survey practice was made by Pullara and Walker (1965, p. 404) who noted heavy reliance upon subjective judgement in CI evaluations. They did, however, note that AROR, PP and IRR were all used to some extent, with PP used most once secondary usage (as support to another method) was taken into account. This early finding indicates that non-discounted methods were used more than discounted methods, although formal analysis itself was limited.

Similar early findings (Istvan (1961a) and Christy (1966) in the USA; Meredith (1964, 1965) in Australia) found that usage of formal analysis methods twenty to thirty years ago was limited, with PP being the most used method and DCF almost never used.

Since then, a number of researchers have suggested a trend towards increased use of DCF techniques (see Pike, 1988, p. 341). Klammer (1972, p. 393) found high use of DCF (67 per cent), as did Fremgen (1973, p. 20) with 76 per cent, Gitman and Forrester (1977, p. 69) with 66 per cent, McMahon (1981, p. 18) with 71 per cent and Klammer and Walker (1984, p. 138) with 75 per cent use of DCF technique.

However, there is continued use of non-DCF analysis techniques. Use of non-DCF methods as the *primary* method of analysis has been reported mainly in medium-sized or smaller businesses (Scott, Gray and Bird, 1972; Runyon, 1983; McIntyre and Coulthurst, 1987). Surprisingly, Bavishi (1981) found widespread primary use of non-DCF methods in US-based multinational corporations, and Bailes and McNally (1984) found low DCF use in New Zealand. Payback period (PP) appears to be the most consistently popular of non-DCF methods, despite its theoretical limitations.

Non-DCF techniques have also appeared to play an important ancillary role in analysing CI proposals, with PP especially featuring as a secondary evaluation technique. For example, Gitman and Forrester (1977, p. 68) found that 41 per cent of their respondents used PP in a secondary capacity. Hendricks (1981, p. 23) found 65 per cent secondary PP use, and Pike (1988, p. 346) recorded a 92 per cent incidence of payback being used as a support technique.

Even though the use of non-DCF techniques seems widespread, CI decision-makers still recognize DCF methods as being "better". Internal rate of return (IRR) is most often cited as being "important" (Fremgen, 1973; Pike, 1988), and PP, despite being widely used, appears to have declined in popularity as a primary analysis technique, perhaps due to increasing recognition of its theoretical weaknesses (Petry, 1975; Petty, Scott and Bird, 1975; Rosenblatt and Jucker, 1979).

It seems that, even when survey respondents use DCF methods, they may be calculating the analyses incorrectly. Marsh *et al.* (1988, p. 23) studied three UK organizations, observing that "although all three companies 'used DCF' we noted many 'errors' in the way it was applied". Also, the use of multiple criteria (Petty, Scott and Bird, 1975; Schall, Sundem and Geijsbeek, 1978; Bavishi, 1981; Mills, 1988; Perera, 1988–9) and continued preference for IRR over NPV (Fremgen, 1973; Oblak and Helm, 1980; Mills, 1988) suggest that it may be premature to assert increased "sophistication" in practice.

Although it is uncertain what "sophistication" exists in CI practice, it is interesting to note research work which has explored

the connection between sophistication and organizational performance. Sophisticated CI practice has usually been interpreted as the
use of at least DCF methods, and possibly of OR techniques such
as simulation and LP. Organizational performance has typically
been measured via earnings per share or operating return on assets.
Perhaps surprisingly, the majority of this work (Christy, 1966;
Klammer, 1973; Haka, Gordon and Pinches, 1985; Haka, 1987)
has found no significant relationship between the level of
sophistication in CI techniques used, and firms' performance.[1]
Klammer (1973) even found a *negative* correlation between the use
of sophisticated DCF techniques and operating return on asset
results.

However, along a similar line, Pike (1988) has noted that the
use of sophisticated CI methods does seem to improve an
organization's "capital expenditure effectiveness" (ability to evaluate and control CI), even though this improved CI effectiveness
may not, in itself, influence financial performance. So, while some
authors have suggested that CI practice is becoming increasingly
sophisticated, and that this may promote "effective" CI management, there is considerable doubt as to whether sophisticated
techniques actually contribute to improved financial performance.
In fact, it may be that *poor* performance stimulates efforts to use
better analysis methods; when organizations are doing well, there
is less incentive to change!

Perhaps most insight into the diversity of practice is provided
by indications of *why* respondents use particular analysis methods.
Those using non-DCF methods have done so for reasons of
familiarity (Lilleyman, 1984), industry acceptance (Petry, 1975),
custom (Soldofsky, 1971), ease of use (Petry, 1975) or satisfaction
with current results (Lilleyman, 1984). Others perceive deficiencies
in DCF methods, including a failure to incorporate non-monetary
benefits (Lapsley, 1986), increased environmental uncertainty
(Mills, 1988), risk and unreliable information (Lilleyman, 1984).

Respondents favouring DCF methods value the recognition of
the time value of money or the easy comparison of investment
proposals, applying well to capital intensive companies (Petry,
1975), and providing an edge in increasingly competitive environments (Moore and Reichert, 1983). IRR users justify their choice
in a variety of ways. Levy and Sarnat (1978) and Pike (1982) have
noted that the percentage expression of IRR may have psychological

---

[1] Although Kim (1982) found some support for a positive relationship between
CI sophistication and performance, the degree of association was weaker than he
had expected.

appeal, perhaps because it gives an immediate ranking or it apparently removes the need for a cut-off rate (also reported in Pike, 1982 and Mills, 1988).

Generally, while research exploring the perceptions of CI decision-makers have begun to provide some insight into *why* "sophisticated" methods are (or are not) used, to date this insight, although interesting, is limited and anecdotal. The *ways* in which analysis methods are employed in CI decision-making remain largely unclear.

Non-financial influences on proposal evaluation

Qualitative, or subjective, factors often influence the progress of proposals through CI evaluation. The most apparent of these factors is perhaps the initial categorization of project proposals. Categorizations often correspond to differing perceived reasons for investment, as outlined in Chapter 2.

There is also evidence that the categorization of a CI project can dictate its required rate of return (RRR). McMahon (1981, p. 19) found that 19 per cent of Australian firms surveyed altered the RRR depending on the type of investment, while Runyon (1983, p. 392) found that 80 per cent of small business managers claimed to make similar alterations to RRR. Perera's (1988–9, p. 23) respondents stated that the stage of the project, its technology or its industry would affect the RRR applied to its financial analysis.

As a result of early categorization, some proposals may never enter the formal evaluation procedures, being judged instead by non-financial criteria. Petty, Scott and Bird (1975) noted that only 47 per cent of their respondents analysed most (80 per cent to 100 per cent) of their capital expenditure proposals, and Lilleyman (1984) later noted that only 51 per cent of his Australian respondents evaluated all capital projects, with 84 per cent evaluating at least half.

For those CI proposals which *are* formally analysed, a number of authors have suggested that projects often have predetermined outcomes. Petty, Scott and Bird (1975, p. 161) noted that the first screening of proposals usually takes place at the point of inception. It has been suggested that, from there, project proposals continue to accumulate commitment until they have become "sales document[s] from a united front" (Marsh *et al.*, 1988, p. 6). Emmanuel, Otley and Merchant (1990, p. 327) comment in a similar vein that "by the time authorization is requested, the acceptability of the project to the originator plus a large section of the organization has already been determined". This hardly forms a basis for objective, financial analysis at the "analysis and acceptance" stage of the CI decision!

Hence, formal financial analysis is perhaps less important in shaping the investment decision than is suggested by prescriptive CI theory. Non-financial criteria are clearly influential in the decision process, although the relative weightings of financial and non-financial criteria are not clear. Indeed, Petty, Scott and Bird (1975, p. 166) reported that 77 per cent of their respondents considered quantitative factors *dominant* in making CI decisions, while Pike (1983b) observed that qualitative factors are considered to be of *almost equal importance* to quantitative factors. Brigham (1975) had suggested that quantitative factors are given more weight where expansion of existing products was considered (Singer, 1985, produced similar results in New Zealand), and "where cashflow data are uncertain, more weight is given to 'judgement'" (p. 22).

Exploring this issue, several researchers have tried to identify the non-financial criteria which influence the selection of CI projects. Fremgen (1973, p. 23) noted that projects were sometimes approved for non-financial reasons including safety, continuation of existing programmes and social, legal or contractual reasons. Petty, Scott and Bird (1975) added environmental issues and employee morale and safety, while Runyon (1983, p. 394) reported the perceived importance of maintaining competitive position and outputs, and government regulation.

Much of the literature on CI analysis asserts that the trend is towards greater sophistication. Even so, many projects proceed without analysis, analysis outcomes are often "pre-ordained" by subjective pre-screening, and qualitative factors are often a substantial influence on the investment decision. Hence, the picture of CI analysis in practice remains uncertain and incomplete.

Determination of cashflow data and required rate of return

The determination of project cashflows and the required rate of return (RRR) criteria are central to CI analysis. Few authors have explored this issue; those who have offer little insight into the practicalities of estimating future, uncertain cashflows.

Schall, Sundem and Geijsbeek (1978, p. 283) noted that "the most common method of predicting cashflows is to first predict net income and then adjust this for non-cash items such as depreciation". This approach may reflect reluctance to take a cashflow view of investment appraisal. In his survey of New Zealand companies, McNally (1980) found that only 32 per cent of respondents always prepared cashflow projections for CI projects, while 15 per cent of respondents rarely or never did so. The remainder prepared cashflow projections frequently or sometimes.

It would seem from this minimal and dated evidence, that cashflow data is problematic in CI analysis. Indeed, the definition and estimation of cashflows is often cited as one of the most critical and difficult stages (Fremgen, 1973; Gitman and Forrester, 1977; Lilleyman, 1984). This reflects perceived practical difficulties in determining cashflow estimates, and the uncertainty inherent in the data used.

The required rate of return (RRR), or "hurdle" or "discount" rate, is explored to only a limited extent in the literature. Prescriptive CI literature refers to market measures of cost of capital such as the CAPM model (see Brealey and Myers, 1991, pp. 161–8 for a discussion of CAPM) as an indicator of a minimum RRR. Some weighted average of the cost of all capital sources (WACC) is often recommended as a yardstick for assessing CIs, as quantified by the appropriate DCF analysis technique (see Keown *et al.*, 1985, pp. 432–40 for a discussion of WACC concepts and usage).

One of the earliest documentations of RRR determination practice is provided by Pullara and Walker (1965), who found frequent use of an arbitrary cut-off rate – usually some measure of PP or an RRR. There was no indication that any organizations were considering RRRs based on average accounting returns or WACC. Since then unsophisticated measures such as historical rates or arbitrary management determinations (or "gut feel") have often been reported (Soldofsky, 1971; Brigham, 1975; Petry, 1975; Petty, Scott and Bird, 1975; Runyon, 1983; Perera, 1988–9). Also, Marsh *et al.* (1988) found recently that cut-off discount rates often appeared arbitrary, even in the three large, seemingly "sophisticated" UK organizations which they studied.

However, there appears to be a growing use of theoretically recommended methods of RRR determination. WACC use is often reported, although authors disagree as to the extent of its use. Brigham (1975) reported 61 per cent of WACC, in the same year that Petry (1975) found 34 per cent and Petty, Scott and Bird (1975) found 30 per cent use of WACC. Later, higher usage of WACC was reported (for example, 54 per cent by Oblak and Helm, 1980, p. 39, 45 per cent by Hendricks, 1981, p. 27, and 63 per cent by McMahon, 1981, p. 20). More recent research has found evidence of CAPM approaches to RRR determination (Perera, 1988–9), perhaps reflecting growing sophistication.

Other theoretically recommended RRR treatments include the use of differential RRRs for different project types or risk profiles, and the regular updating of RRRs. Survey evidence for both is inconsistent. In 1975 Brigham claimed that over half the US firms he surveyed adjusted RRRs according to risk (see also Petry, 1975), while Petty, Scott and Bird (1975) found that only one-third of respondents used more than one RRR. Oblak and Helm (1980), McMahon (1981) and Baker (1981) later recorded higher use of multiple RRRs, although inconsistent categorizations of RRRs make comparison difficult.

It appears generally that RRRs are not often updated. Brigham found that 39 per cent of his respondents revised RRRs less than once a year, with 32 per cent making irregular revisions. Pike (1983b) later found that 61 per cent of surveyed organizations regularly reviewed the RRR, although the definition of "regular" is unclear, while Runyon (1983, p. 392) found that only 17 per cent of small businesses surveyed undertook "frequent" revisions of RRR.

Ross (1986) made an interesting observation, that hurdle rates may be published (*de facto*), or actual. That is, the stated hurdle rate may differ from the rate(s) actually used. Sometimes both were the same, indicating a decentralized CI process where uniform RRR criteria were required. Where they have differed, the published rate may have acted as a starting point for considering projects further. In other instances there may have been no set hurdle rate, and projects have simply competed with each other, indicating a capital rationing situation.

Overall, survey research reflects practical difficulties with two major inputs into the formal CI analysis procedure. The prediction of cashflows is little explored, but indications are that cashflow information is rarely reliable. Similarly, the RRR is computed and used in a multitude of ways, often based on judgement or some "pot pourri" of inputs of varying significance. These findings throw into question the formal analysis of CI where it *is* undertaken, and perhaps constitute justification where recommended formal analyses are not undertaken.

Risk analysis and the use of operations research techniques

The risk analysis methods cited in the CI literature take two basic forms. The first entails adjustment of the value assigned to cashflows (lowered), or the RRR (raised), to reflect that a "risky" cashflow is worth less than a "certain" cashflow. This method of accounting for risk is arbitrary, and gives little appreciation of the range of possible outcomes from a CI.

The second form of risk analysis is borrowed from the operations research (OR) literature, and involves the assignment of probabilities to possible outcomes, producing a range of results which can be evaluated for acceptability (as outlined by Hertz, 1964).

There is little provision in the CI literature for dealing with uncertainty. It is generally assumed that some assignation of probability to known variables can be made, or that the financial results of a CI can be estimated. Little help is offered where there is complete uncertainty about the nature or impact of variables affecting a CI project. Perhaps the best approach to coping with uncertainty is the use of simulation techniques, although they do not appear to be used widely in practice.

In the literature, several aspects of risk treatment in CI practice have been considered: the frequency with which organizations undertake risk analysis, the ways in which riskiness is ascertained, the modifications made to analyses to account for perceived risk, and the use of OR techniques.

Pullara and Walker (1965, p. 406) were among the earliest researchers to investigate risk consideration in CI practice. They found some firms (32 per cent) using different RRRs for differing risk levels, 50 per cent using some other method of adjustment (including judgement) and others (18 per cent) recognizing that they did not incorporate risk into their CI analyses.

Since then, varying reports of risk analysis have emerged. It must be recognized that authors have used differing definitions of "sophisticated" analysis, so for this review sophisticated risk treatment will be taken as any attempt to quantify risk-adjusted cashflows. Using this definition, sophisticated risk adjustment has been recorded for between 15 per cent and 50 per cent of respondents. Fremgen (1973, p. 23) found a 32 per cent incidence of sophisticated risk adjustment, Petry (1975, p. 64) recorded 26 per cent, and Patterson (1989, p. 82) found a 47 per cent use of adjusted cashflows in his New Zealand survey.

Research reveals that risk adjustment is often subjective. For example, Bavishi (1981) recorded that 60 per cent of his respondents "subjectively" altered RRRs (see also Petry, 1975; Gitman and Forrester, 1977; Oblak and Helm, 1980; Runyon, 1983). It seems that exercising judgement is the only way in which many capital budgeters adjust for perceived risk; there are many more who do nothing.

Some researchers have speculated as to the type of organization which may place higher emphasis on risk adjustment. Kim and Farragher (1981) observed that lower-risk companies used risk analysis more, and suggested that analysis may reduce risk (although they did not consider the possibility that risk analysis was perceived as less valuable, and was thus less frequently performed, in high-uncertainty environments). Oblak and Helm (1980) observed frequent risk assessment in multinational corporations, and Runyon (1983, p. 393) observed ". . . the use of less sophisticated measures as small businessmen attempt to deal with the element of risk".

There have been few attempts to determine the ways in which CI risk is ascertained, and they have generally identified the same few methods. Petty, Scott and Bird (1975, pp. 166–7) referred to respondents' definitions of risk, which were mostly concerned with achieving a target return or variation in returns. This led the authors to note that "variance is coming into its own as a concept of risk". Yet, Singer (1985, p. 35) found that "New Zealand managers are less inclined than their US counterparts to construe 'risk' in distributional terms . . . and more likely to think in terms of specific threats or potential weaknesses".

Schall, Sundem and Geijsbeek (1978) reported more sophisticated risk assessment, including probability distributions of cashflows, sensitivity analyses, and measures of covariance with other projects. However, they also recognized frequent subjective risk assessment, or total ignoring of risk. Later Perera (1988–9, p. 23) noted high use of subjective risk measures (six out of eleven, or 55 per cent of organizations studied). Some respondents used only quantitative measures (27 per cent), or both (18 per cent).

Similar inconsistency can be observed with respect to how (if at all) risk is adjusted for in CI analyses. Most respondents cite subjective adjustment of criteria (e.g. increasing required ARORs, reduction in PP or increasing the RRR), or some alteration to cashflows. Others have employed more sophisticated certainty equivalent or probabilistic treatments of cashflows (Fremgen, 1973; Petty, Scott and Bird, 1975; Gitman and Forrester, 1977), sensitivity analysis and simulation (McMahon, 1981).

What emerges from the literature is that risk analysis is not often recognized or performed in the way that textbooks dictate. Where riskiness *is* recognized, it is often accounted for subjectively. Where attempts are made at quantifying risk and its effect on investments, a variety of techniques are used.

The use of OR techniques is not known with any certainty. Klammer (1972, p. 392) reported that the use of OR techniques had increased since the early 1960s, the most popular being probability theory, simulation, PERT/CPM and LP. However, nothing was said of the way in which such methods were used, or the weighting given to their results. Fremgen (1973) identified LP as an emerging technique under conditions of capital rationing, noting that although 17 per cent of respondents had used LP regularly, he expected to observe higher use in ten to twenty years' time as the technology became more widespread.

However, recent evidence has suggested that Fremgen was somewhat optimistic. Pike and Sharp (1989, p. 137) reported slow increases in the use of LP,[2] from 11 per cent in 1975 up to 21 per cent in 1986. Of this 21 per cent, over half used LP only "rarely", and LP was used predominantly by large companies (with CI budgets of over £50 million). Although Pike and Sharp noted (p. 137) "a significant association between the degree of usage of nearly all management science techniques and the extent to which computer software is applied to investment decisions", even with increased availability of computers they predicted only a 29 per cent use of LP by 1991. The reasons for this slow adoption of LP methods are unclear, although Pike and Sharp (p. 140) suggest that better software and improved training of managers are required to bring about greater acceptance of OR techniques in general.

Lilleyman (1984) found in Australia that in accounting for risk, 59 per cent of his respondents used sensitivity analysis, 36 per cent probability analysis, and 32 per cent simulation. One year earlier, Moore and Reichert (1983, p. 638) had concluded that the frequent use of OR tools is strongly associated with the use of sophisticated CI methods, although Pike and Wolfe (1988, p. 78) found in their 1986 UK study that "management science techniques . . . are in the majority of cases not used". More recently, Ho and Pike (1991, p. 236) have noted that "larger-sized UK organisations . . . prefer relatively simple risk adjustment and sensitivity analysis . . .". The authors observed that "advanced risk analysis techniques . . . are still in an experimental stage in practice", and that "simple approaches tend not to be replaced by the more advanced ones, but are used to supplement analysis".

So, evidence for the extent of use of sophisticated risk analysis methods is mixed, but suggests that there is a considerable gap between theory (and theoretical applications of OR approaches) and practice.

---

[2] Pike and Sharp (1989) do not refer explicitly to LP, but "mathematical programming" can be assumed to have similar meaning.

It could be said that many aspects of the practice of risk assessment are still largely undocumented. Despite numerous reports of increasing use of risk analysis, little is known of the way in which risk information is gathered, the use of the analysis methods, or the way in which their output is taken into account. Risk treatment would seem to warrant greater exploration as part of the CI process.

Analysis and acceptance: summary

The emphasis in the literature on analysis and acceptance of CI proposals could indicate that either analysis and acceptance is perceived as most important in CI, or it has proven to be easiest to research. Perhaps a combination of the two is true. However, clear gaps remain in understanding practice. Although the stated trend has been towards greater use of "sophisticated" methods (despite frequent evidence to the contrary), the ways in which these methods are used is largely unexplored. Also, the relative importance of financial and non-financial measures is unclear; once known, it may support the claim by some authors (e.g. King, 1975; Mukherjee and Henderson, 1987) that the past preoccupation with formal financial analysis and acceptance practice may be misguided.

POST AUDIT

The majority of post audit research has been concerned with the proportion of firms undertaking some kind of post audit procedure. In 1972 Klammer observed that 88 per cent of firms surveyed claimed to conduct post audit. He compared this to similar surveys as early as 1959, which had found 50 per cent use of post audit, and asserted that this represented significant growth (Mukherjee and Henderson (1987) later made similar assertions). However, Klammer did not attempt to ascertain the nature of these post audits or the way in which their results impacted upon the CI process.

In comparison to Klammer, Pike (1983b) found that post audits on major projects were conducted by only 48 per cent of firms. Lilleyman (1984) found that of the Australian firms surveyed, 22 per cent always conducted post audits and a further 62 per cent sometimes did; however, 13 per cent of those using post audit stated that even where significant variations were discovered, no action was taken. Clearly, there is inconsistency in the findings relating to post audit procedures.

In 1981, Scapens and Sale considered post audit in greater depth than Klammer had earlier. These authors noted (p. 409) reasons given by UK capital budgeters for *not* undertaking post audit, stating that "it is sometimes thought . . . that it is impracticable to review CI projects after they have been implemented . . . . These difficulties have led many UK corporation controllers to reject the idea . . .". Pike (1983b) also reported perceptions of adequate control at the spending stage, difficulties in isolating costs and benefits of "live" projects and perceived questionable value of post audits.

Scapens and Sale (p. 409) identified (but unfortunately did not explain), the differing adoption of post audit in the USA. They noted that ". . . in the US post-completion audits gained acceptance in the late 1950s", and reported that 84 per cent of US respondents conducted post audits, compared to only 36 per cent in the UK.

They went on to consider why post audits are seen as useful, quoting a divisional controller (p. 410): "since introducing post-completion audits we have found a substantial improvement in project proposals . . . the effect [of post completion-audits] is mainly psychological." This indicates that the utility of post audit is not so much in identifying errors, but in the incentive for project initiators to do a "better" job of the proposal, so that post audit is less likely to reveal inconsistencies for which the initiator may be held responsible (see also Pike, 1983b).

It appears that most capital budgeters using post audits do not review all projects – normally a selection is made. Scapens and Sale (p. 410) note that "sometimes the selection is random . . . and other times it is based on the size of the projects". Pike (1983b) later made similar observations. Again, it appears that the apparent random selection of projects for post audit motivates more careful project initiation. Scapens and Sale (1981) found that responsibility for post audit is divided almost equally between corporate headquarters and the division itself. The timing of audits varied, but was most often after realization of revenues from the project.

There has been some attempt to relate the use of post audit to characteristics of the firm, particularly size, although with limited success. Pike (1983b) concluded that the use of post audit did not appear related to firm size, while McIntyre and Coulthurst (1987) observed that more medium-sized firms consider post audit important than do larger firms. No clear relationships have emerged in this, or any other, facet of post audit research. This important later stage of the CI process has been largely disregarded, and as a result there remains much to be learned of its use in practice.

ORGANIZATIONAL PERSONNEL

Research considering organizational personnel has mainly identified who is involved in CI. One little-documented aspect is the role of technical (e.g. engineering) staff as compared to management accounting (or finance) staff in formulating and assessing investment proposals.

Mukherjee and Henderson (1987, p. 81) noted that the budget development phase (where much early screening takes place) involved engineers and accountants more than finance personnel. McNally (1980) had previously found in New Zealand that the use of engineering studies to estimate costs had fallen by 21 per cent from 1974 to 1978. However, Bower (1970) in his landmark case study of a large US corporation, rejected what he saw as a limited perception of those people who ought to be involved in CI, stating (p. 345) that CI ". . . cannot be accomplished without the integration of the work of many specialists in the context of corporate purpose . . . it is *not* primarily a task for financial staff or for engineers". However, the extent of the actual influence of engineers and other technical personnel is not well documented in the CI research literature.

Other observations about personnel relate to the possible influences of differing education levels. Petry (1975, pp. 64–5) suggested that "the increased use of time-weighted techniques probably has been influenced by the large influx of recent college graduates who are familiar with these techniques and their advantages".

Soldofsky (1971, pp. 28–9) despaired of small business managers' ignorance of CI analysis methods. He noted that not a single respondent to his questionnaire had understood the relevance of life expectancy to a capital purchase's rate of return, and that only 10 per cent of respondents calculated payback period correctly. Such findings illustrate the importance of considering personnel factors when interpreting CI practice.

Survey respondents generally refer to a CI committee, CEO or board of directors as carrying the final responsibility for making CI decisions. Scapens and Sale (1981, p. 403) noted that "some writers . . . have argued that corporate management lack the expertise to evaluate individual divisional proposals and generally, do no more than suggest minor alterations . . .". Their suggestion was that higher managerial levels served only to monitor decisions which "for all practical purposes had already been taken". However, Scapens and Sale also noted (pp. 406–7) that the freedom of lower managers was restricted by the need to correspond to strategic decisions previously taken at corporate level.

Recently, Butler *et al.* (1991, p. 404) reported on case studies of three UK organizations, where they observed that "middle management . . . are the people who get most involved in the implementation of investment decisions . . . higher management will tend to see a given project against a background of a number of other projects [and] lower-level people will tend to be experts offering advice but without direct responsibility for the decision". Hence, although some general framework may exist within an organization, as Mukherjee and Henderson (1987, p. 81) note, "just who *is* making the capital investment decisions is unclear".

Another personnel issue is the subjectivity of CI decision-making, and the potential influence of individual and organizational politics. Bower (1970) observed that personnel can significantly affect the way that a decision is handled, since "the managers who make the individual investment and/or planning decisions respond to unique and personal sets of incentives. These incentives are not necessarily or likely to be the same as those of managers at any other place in the organization".

Mukherjee and Henderson (1987, pp. 81 and 85) later noted that

> experience with a project's sponsor, the project initiator's previous track record and interdepartmental politics all affect the credibility of cashflow predictions . . . in contrast to theoretical assumptions, many projects are rejected during the preselection stages apparently for non-economic considerations (for example, personalities and interdepartmental politics).

Ross (1986, p. 18) provides a good example of the influence of personalities, noting a case where a project which did not meet the required IRR criterion is accepted because the plant manager is considered ". . . cautious in his proposals and is very effective in other respects".

Such personality factors no doubt play a part in many aspects of organizational life. What is interesting is that they are largely assumed away or ignored in the CI research literature, once again rendering an incomplete picture of the complexities of practice.

Reward and evaluation of employees also needs to be considered.

Bower (1970, p. 279) noted the importance of "formal organization, salary review, bonus plans and the accounting systems" in
encouraging active participation in CI. However, research suggests
that the criteria used for evaluation may often be incongruent
with sophisticated CI appraisal techniques.

Moore and Reichert (1983) found that performance was evaluated
by profit and return on investment measures by virtually all their
survey respondents. Mukherjee and Henderson's (1987, p. 85)
findings were similar, leading them to note that "ROI-type
measures are the most frequently reported basis of performance
measurement . . . [which is] . . . inconsistent with the use of DCF
techniques for selection". Scapens and Sale (1981, p. 396) noted
that there was "no suggestion . . . that cashflow accounting is
replacing profit measurement to any great extent", even though
this would improve the performance measurement problem.

As Scapens and Sale (1981, p. 391) noted, performance measures
should be consistent with organizational goals. If we are to
presume that these goals are to maximize shareholders' wealth,
then the evaluation criteria indicated by Moore and Reichert and
Mukherjee and Henderson will fail to promote "rational" decision-
making.

The limited research attention given to organizational personnel
in the CI process has served only to highlight possible areas for
further investigation. Little is known of the influence of the people
behind the process, or the implications of behavioural issues for
CI theory.

STRATEGIC PLANNING

Although there is a large literature on corporate goal-setting, the
incorporation of such strategic goals into CI has been considered
to only a limited extent. Mukherjee and Henderson (1987, p. 85)
noted that strategic planning was a problem area of CI theory.
They stated that "our review of the related literature leads us to
believe that much of the gap [between theory and practice] can
be attributed to deficiences in the theory itself", including an
"inability to incorporate strategic considerations". Pike (1983b,
p. 201) also questioned the focus of theory, quoting a practitioner's
criticism:[3] "investment decision-making could be improved significantly if the emphasis were placed on asking the appropriate
strategic questions rather than on increasing the sophistication of

---

[3] From Hastie (1974, p. 36).

measurement techniques". Marsh *et al.* (1988, p. 17) observed in their UK case study research that planning division personnel could exercise "an indirect influence, by helping specify and predefine the kinds of projects which came up, through encouraging the submission of projects consistent with group strategy". So here we see evidence of strategic planning impacting upon CI "idea generation", although the impact is "indirect" rather than explicit.

There is some evidence to suggest that corporate goals (as with personnel evaluation) may not always be congruent with the "rational" objectives of CI. In 1975 Petty, Scott and Bird explored the perceived importance of corporate goals and found that maximization of return on assets and growth in earnings per share were by far the most significant. Patterson (1989, p. 77) later reviewed subsequent considerations of corporate goals (Petty and Scott, 1981; Stanley and Block, 1984) together with his own New Zealand survey results, to conclude that:

> maximisation of accounting rates of return is the primary objective of both US and New Zealand firms, with maximisation of earnings per share growth a close second. Maximisation of the value of shareholders' wealth . . . generally ranks in third to fifth position . . . despite its primary importance in the normative theory of finance.

Perhaps corporate orientation toward such goals has impacted upon the way in which CI takes place.

One aspect of long-term corporate decision-making which clearly impacts upon CI behaviour is the availability of financing for CI, or the imposition of capital rationing. Pike (1983a, p. 663), refers to the work of Levy and Sarnat (1982), noting that rationing is not exclusive to capital, but "applies equally to non-capital constraints such as the supply of key personnel to manage, or the capacity of senior management to approve and review, additional major projects". However, capital rationing is the most considered form of constraint in the literature.

Pike (1983, p. 664) noted that capital rationing is often internally imposed, and asserted that "motivation for such a policy which deprives shareholders of both valuable investment returns and the tax subsidy on debt financing is clearly non-financial". The incidence of capital rationing is well documented in the survey literature. Rosenblatt and Jucker (1979, p. 66) provide one of the earlier reviews of capital rationing noting that "the survey data shows [*sic*] that . . . capital rationing is a common phenomenon among the firms surveyed".

Fremgen (1973, p. 24) recorded reasons for the internal imposition of capital rationing, including management-imposed debt limits, the desire for regular dividends, desired EPS or P/E ratios, restrictions on share issues and inadequate cashflows. Other examples can be found in Gitman and Forrester (1977, p. 69) who found that 69 per cent of their respondents cited self-imposed debt limits, 15 per cent targeted EPS results and 2 per cent desired dividend payouts. Pike (1983a, p. 667) found respondents quoting "unwillingness to increase borrowings" and "economic uncertainty" as reasons for internally-imposed capital rationing. Such findings indicate that managers perceive themselves as having rational justifications for imposing capital rationing, which are likely to support the continuing imposition of restraints upon capital expenditure.

It is apparent that capital rationing is a widespread phenomenon which represents one important way in which corporate goals can be reflected in CI. However, capital rationing is normally considered to be incongruent to the theoretical basis of sophisticated CI analysis tools, and so corporate strategy in this instance may impede the use of DCF analysis techniques.

It is not known with any certainty just how strong the relationship between corporate strategy and CI is. Yet, Pike and Wolfe (1988, p. 36) suggest that "increasingly firms are recognising that investment decisions should be made within the strategic context". Researchers must further explore this "context" and its implications if a complete picture of CI decision-making is to emerge.

CONCLUSIONS

When the empirical CI literature is examined, it is clear that there remain gaps in understanding practice. The survey research reveals only *stated* practice – the practice that survey respondents would have researchers believe occurs. However, individual respondents cannot speak for all organizational personnel, and they may feel compelled to represent the practice of their organization as being structured and "rational" (within their own perceptions of what this means) when in fact it may not be so (see Rappaport, 1979).

However, it is not difficult to identify areas where little has been learnt. The less quantifiable aspects of CI – those of idea generation, personnel considerations and links to strategic planning – remain largely unexplored. Even those thoroughly researched aspects (such as the use of DCF analysis techniques) have produced confusing results, suggesting that we may not know as much about practice as many researchers would like to believe.

Also, there is substantial evidence to suggest that CI decision-making may not occur in a rational, orderly fashion as suggested by the typical "model" identified and discussed in Chapter 2. Case study research in particular has revealed "political" and "social" models of decision-making which do not correspond to traditional notions of an economically motivated, rational choice process.

This chapter, together with Chapter 2, exposes the "theory–practice" gap which has characterized CI decision-making literature and research. In the next chapter, this gap is explored, as alternative conceptions of CI decision-making are proposed and discussed in relation to both traditional CI models and the evidence from empirical research.

Problems

1. With reference to Figure 2.1 on p. 10, "A capital investment model", which stage(s) of the CI "process" have been given the most attention in the empirical research literature? Why do you think this is?
2. Would you say that the research evidence demonstrates increasing adoption of "sophisticated" CI analysis techniques in practice? Why, or why not?
3. On p. 118 a practitioner's comment, made many years ago, was quoted:

    investment decision-making could be improved significantly if the emphasis were placed on asking the appropriate strategic questions rather than on increasing the sophistication of measurement techniques

    (Hastie, 1974, p. 36)

    Discuss your reaction to this statement, taking into account the empirical research which has occurred in recent years.
4. In some instances, survey results from different countries have produced quite different indications of CI practice. Identify an example of this from this chapter, and suggest possible reasons why results from different countries might not agree.
5. Can you identify any aspects of CI practice which do not appear to be well explained by the "process" characterization of CI decision-making? If so, what are they, and why do you consider them to differ from what the "process model" might suggest for practice?

6. In the Appendix to this book (p. 186) there is an illustration
    of CI proposal forms (these are based closely on the actual
    forms of a large company).
    Discuss the strengths and weaknesses of these documents for
    practical use in CI decision-making.

7

Capital Investment as a Human Decision-Making Activity: a Behavioural Perspective

INTRODUCTION

Recall that the CI decision-making "process" model presented in Chapter 2 was based on a rational economics perspective of the objectives and activity of CI decision-making. This perspective has also dominated the development of normative CI theory and the techniques and approaches presented in Chapters 3 to 5.

However, after reviewing what is known about CI practice in Chapter 6, it is clear that there is an apparent "theory–practice gap". Many CI decision-makers continue to use "unsophisticated" approaches to analysing CI projects and there appears to be limited attention given to other stages of the CI process, such as idea generation and post audit review.

Many academics have grappled with the question of why this theory–practice gap may exist. Are practitioners ignorant of the sophisticated advances in the techniques available for CI analysis? Do they not have time to undertake such analyses? Is the appropriate information not available? There has been limited empirical support for all these propositions. But, despite increased awareness of these issues, still normative models of the CI process fail to adequately describe or inform practice. Something is missing. An important aspect of CI decision-making which is undoubtedly contributing to the theory–practice gap is identified and explored in this chapter.

It is often forgotten that CI decision-making is a *human* activity rather than an objective, mechanical procedure. There are people behind the "process". It is this human appreciation of CI decision-making which appears to be missing from the rational, economic models which have driven normative CI theory. Theory has reflected an implicit image of economically rational, profit-maximizing decision-makers with perfect knowledge and few emotions. Such people can correctly use and interpret the sophisticated CI techniques proposed in the literature, and will never make a bad decision simply because they're having a bad day! A hopeful, but somewhat unrealistic scenario.

Further behavioural factors, both at an individual and organizational level, impact on CI decision-making practice, and contribute to our observation of a theory–practice gap. These factors must be considered so that a complete, rich picture of CI decision-making can be achieved.

In this chapter we will first examine what is meant by "rationality". This concept underpins decision-making theory, and we will see that perhaps a limited notion of "rationality" has directed our understanding of CI decision-making. There are other notions of rationality which may be relevant to understanding CI in practice. Then, the differing "roles" of accounting (and CI) information are explored. It is suggested that the information flowing from CI analyses can be used in a number of different ways to serve a number of different purposes. Some insight into these various uses of accounting information is useful for understanding the complexity of CI decision-making practice.

Specific aspects of organizational activity (performance evaluation and motivation, and strategic planning) are then focused upon to illustrate ways in which CI decisions shape, and are shaped by, other aspects of organizational and behavioural context. Finally, we reflect upon the implications of behavioural issues for understanding CI practice, and improving CI theory. The aim of this chapter is to give the reader a richer contextual understanding of CI decision-making (in theory and in practice) and of the "roles" of financial analyses in supporting CI decision-making.

WHAT IS "RATIONALITY"?

The capital investment activity is about making decisions. It is usually assumed that, when making decisions, people act "rationally"; but what does this mean? The answer to this question has important implications for considering the theory–practice gap in capital investment decision-making, and for suggesting ways in which practice can (if necessary) be improved. The techniques available to capital investment decision-makers are designed to assist "rational" decision-making. But, if the decision-maker's notion of rationality differs from that which is implicit in the technique, then a mismatch occurs. We may not observe recommended techniques being used in practice, if the techniques are not effective in supporting the "rational" motives of the decision-maker.

The economics roots of capital investment theory have brought with them an implicit perspective of rationality. Economic decision-makers are presumed to define and order goals, to foresee all possible courses of action, to anticipate all possible outcomes from these actions and to make a "rational" choice of action which will optimize the attainment of the predetermined goals (Lindblom, 1968). Hollis and Nell (1975, pp. 53–4) paint an amusing picture of this "rational economic man":

> He lurks in the assumptions leading an enlightened existence between input and output, stimulus and response . . . . We do not know what he wants. But we do know that, whatever it is, he will maximize ruthlessly to get it . . . .. As producer he maximises market-share or profit. As consumer he maximises utility by omniscient and improbable comparison of, for instance, marginal strawberries with marginal cement . . . . Unlike the man in the street, he never misses an opening, ignores a price change, overrates the short-run or turns a blind eye to the unquantifiable.

Few would argue that the economic model of decision-making "rationality" bears any resemblance to the nature and environment of the human decision-maker. Indeed Cooper (1975, pp. 199–200) noted that "firms' disregard for formal methods of investment appraisal is based on the suggestion that the behaviour of a firm may be inconsistent with the economist's concept of rationality in decision taking". Others too have observed the limitations of rational economics in explaining human decision-making practice (for example, Churchman, 1968; Hosseini, 1990).

In CI decision-making, the recommended DCF analysis models reflect the assumption that the decision-maker's goal is to maximize the "wealth" generation of each CI, and that this will in turn maximize total organizational wealth. Of course, each individual decision-maker has his or her own goals. These may range from maximizing personal remuneration to enhancing job security, or seeking status and power. The pursuit of these goals by a CI decision-maker may not contribute to the maximization of organizational wealth. Therefore, a goal incongruence problem can arise – what is best for the individual may not be best for the organization as a whole.

This dilemma will be further explored later in this chapter, but for now, consider a simple example. A management accountant is responsible for making a recommendation regarding the purchase of a new computer-based decision support system (DSS). This system, if purchased, would reduce the need for the management accounting division to collect information and produce reports. Such reports would be automatically generated by the DSS. The purchase of this system may be perceived as threatening the security of the management accounting division, thus undermining the status and security of the management accountant's position. Although the DSS is a financially attractive project, would you expect the management accountant to recommend its purchase? Such conflicts of interest illustrate the potential for confounding the CI decision-making activity.

Even if we could assume that the CI decision-maker chooses to act first and foremost in the interests of organizational wealth maximization, recommended DCF models impose daunting requirements. To determine an appropriate required rate of return, the decision-maker must be able to ascertain future opportunity costs, riskiness (or volatility) of an investment's cashflows and some expectation of future costs of capital. Similarly, DCF models require that the decision-maker has a reasonable idea of the future cashflows from a capital investment, or at least an appreciation of the range of likely cashflows.

The estimation of future cashflows is particularly problematic, for two reasons. First, future events are uncertain. Unless gifted with supernatural powers, few CI decision-makers can foresee the future! Indeed, Hogarth and Makridakis note that:

> considerable misconceptions exist concerning the ability of economists and business forecasters to predict important changes either in the general level of economic activity or for a given industry, firm or product . . . forecasters and planners have shown systematic deficiencies in their predictions and plans for the future.
>
> (1981, p. 123)

Gimpl and Dakin (1984) went even further, suggesting that often management's fascination for forecasting is a manifestation of anxiety-relieving superstitious behaviour, with the same basic function as magical rites! Perhaps not all forecasting efforts are intended to serve this purpose, but the fact is that forecasting of cashflows is an uncertain business. Brealey and Myers (1984, p. 223) give a good example of forecasting difficulties:

> a study by one company of 50 projects showed that the actual present value of "cost reduction" projects was 10 per cent above the forecast whereas for "sales expansion" projects the actual present value was 40 per cent below the forecast and for "the products" it was 90 per cent below.

This certainly brings into question the ability to people to "foresee all possible outcomes from alternative actions", a skill expected of the economically rational decision-maker.

A second difficulty with estimating cashflows for CI appraisal lies with the behaviour of decision-makers. Hogarth and Makridakis (1981, p. 127) outline aspects of human judgement which reduce decision-makers' ability to assimilate accurate information. Examples include a tendency of decision-makers to "retain information selectively in accord with their prejudices, and to reject possible disconfirming evidence". Similarly, people tend to assume that more information is better and leads to improved quality of decisions, even though some of this information may be redundant. These and other behavioural decision-making tendencies noted by Hogarth and Makridakis lead to biased forecasts of cashflows, which are erroneously accepted as being sufficiently supported.

Operations research techniques such as simulation, LP and sensitivity analysis can provide a framework for dealing with the unstructured environment in which many CI decisions are made. yet, they cannot remove the problem of uncertainty. In order to use OR techniques, the decision-maker must still be able to quantify future events, eliminate uncertainty, and make "rational" NPV maximizing decisions. The basic practical problems still remain.

Recognizing that problems exist in translating decision-making theories into practice, it is necessary to look beyond the dominant theoretical perspective of "economic rationality". Research suggests that practice does not reflect textbook theories of how people should make CI decisions, and it is not helpful to our understanding simply to dismiss practice as somehow ill-formed or incorrect. To appreciate the needs and motives of CI decision-makers in practice, we must seek alternative explanations of what might be considered rational in CI decision-making.

Rationality is a concept which has received substantial attention in the sociological literature.[1] The most significant contribution to sociological discussions of rationality is the work of Max Weber. Weber (1961) saw "rationality" as a highly specialized form of thinking which develops around clusters of activity. He suggested that commerce, as one such cluster of activity, produces its own rationality. Hence, Weber saw rationality as contextual, depending upon the "cluster of activity" of which the actor was a part, and the socialization which had occurred to include the actor in that "cluster".

The formation of professional accounting bodies could be seen as an example of this "cluster" formation. Members of such a professional body become socialized into codes of conduct and group expectations which dictate appropriate behaviours for achieving commonly agreed objectives. That is, "rational" behaviour for a professional accountant is influenced by the context of professional expectations.

A useful starting point in considering how decision-making practice can be affected by such "contextual rationality" is offered by the work of Allison (1969). Allison produced a landmark analysis of the Cuban missile crisis, providing a framework for considering group decision-making which has since been emulated in many decision-making literatures, including the accounting literature. Allison identified three modes of decision-making:

1. A "rational policy model" which interprets decisions as "reasonable" choices made by "actors", given known objectives – i.e. action is a calculated response to a problem.
2. An "organizational process model" which views decisions as the output of organizations, given particular organizational contexts, pressures, procedures and "repertoires".
3. A "governmental politics model" which interprets decisions as a result of bargaining games which are influenced by perceptions, motivations, positions, powers and manoeuvres of the political adversaries involved.

Traditional approaches to CI decision-making clearly fall into the first of the decision-making modes identified by Allison. The CI decision-maker is expected to know his or her objectives, and to

---

[1] Increasingly, management accounting researchers are looking to the sociological literature for insight into the "social" behaviour of people within organizations.

"calculate" a response to a decision problem. However, as Allison notes, organizations have their own contexts, pressures and procedures. Therefore, it is conceivable to expect that CI decisions are influenced by these pressures and expectations, as they are made acceptable within the organizational "culture" and context.

It is equally conceivable that political forces are at play in many organizations! Many CI decision-makers may be cognisant of their own "bargaining" positions and will make "rational" decisions which are consistent with advancing their personal goals within the organization. This suggestion is supported by Mukherjee and Henderson (1987, pp. 81 and 85) who noted that "many projects are rejected at the preselection stages [of the CI decision], apparently for non-economic considerations (for example, personalities and interdepartmental politics)".

An interesting extension to the alternative decision-making perspectives introduced by Allison is offered by Jones (1989). Jones proposes a "socio-rational model" which combines a range of concepts of rationality: objective rationality, subjective rationality, intersubjective rationality, and positional rationality. (See Northcott, 1991, for a further discussion of Jones's socio-rational model as it relates to capital investment.)

The "objective rationality" identified by Jones can be seen to relate to traditional economics notions of capital investment decision-making. Jones (1989, p. 24) noted that, within this form of rationality:

> information is seen as a matter of presenting . . . facts through the use of techniques which are themselves capable of universalistic validation . . . . The validation of such techniques is concerned with their logic, rigour, internal consistency, accuracy, reliability, relevance and so on. *Hence a technique which recognises the time-value of money is preferred as more rigorous than one that does not*
> . . . .(Emphasis added.)

Capital investment theory, and its focus on the use of sophisticated techniques, appears to fit well Jones's definition of objective rationality. These techniques have been refined and modified to make them more rigorous and "reliable". Yet still, many organizations have problems with making CI decisions. Jones (1989, pp. 25–9) notes the need to look beyond this narrow rationality. He suggests that action (and decisions) can be understood in technical, personal, social and political terms, at the same moment.

The implication for CI decision-making of considering alternative perspectives on "rationality" is interesting. We may now accept that decision-makers who do not use "sophisticated" CI analysis practices (as prescribed in textbooks) are not necessarily acting irrationally. They may simply be advancing another type of "rationality" over that which we have come to expect from rational economics. Fifteen years ago, if a timber company had elected to invest in planting fast-growing, renewable forests rather than to mill readily available rainforests, their decision might have been perceived as economically irrational. But today's social and political climate would indicate that this decision might have been in the best long-term business interests of the company. Perhaps such a decision taken fifteen years ago would now be viewed as far-sighted, rather than economically suicidal? Rationality is contextual.

This alternative view of rationality in CI decision-making does not negate the need for sophisticated CI analysis methods. Indeed, they may often play a key role in allowing decision-makers to pursue *any* of the forms of "rationality" outlined above. However, it is important to get a realistic perspective of the role of CI analysis techniques in the overall decision-making activity. While the techniques can produce numerical "answers", the ways in which these "answers" are used by decision-makers in advancing preferred courses of action can differ.

Recall from Chapter 6 that studies of the relationship between firm performance and the use of sophisticated CI techniques have revealed a *negative* relationship. This may suggest that poorer-performing firms seek more sophisticated techniques as a panacea for under-achievement. However, there is no convincing evidence that the use of sophisticated techniques alone produces superior CI results. Again, this suggests that the decision-making activity surrounds, and extends beyond, the financial analysis of CI proposals – it does not begin and end with the application of sophisticated analysis techniques.

In order for CI analysis techniques to be used appropriately in practice, it is important to consider *why* they are used. Noting that economic rationality may not be the sole driving force in CI decision-making, let us now consider some of the ways in which information from CI analyses may be used.

ALTERNATIVE USES OF ACCOUNTING INFORMATION

Burchell *et al.* (1980) proposed alternative models of how decision-makers may actually use accounting information. Uses of the information resulting from CI analyses can be viewed in much the same way. Chua (1988) refers to eight "roles" of accounting information, identified by Burchell *et al.*:[2]

1. A rational/instrumental role, assisting rational decision-making to achieve optimal decisions for the attainment of organizational objectives (a rational economics perspective).
2. A symbolic role, signalling to others inside and outside the organization that decisions are being taken "rationally".
3. A ritualistic role, legitimating the "irrationalities" of decision-makers by creating rituals to obscure what is happening and to make it more difficult to change what is happening.
4. A mythical role, accepting "myths" by faith as an explanation of reality. Examples of such myths include the "existence" of a corporation, and corporate objectives. "Myths" serve to reduce complex interrelationships to dimensions which are comprehensible to decision-makers.
5. A political/bargaining role, using accounting information to achieve political power or a bargaining advantage.
6. A legitimating/retrospective rationalizing role, justifying decisions that have already been made by affording them "rational" credibility.
7. A disciplinary role, using accounting as a tool of power over subordinates, as it is perceived as representing the "truth".
8. A repressive/dominating/ideological role, alienating workers from management and owners. Accounting becomes a "surveillance system" (Kelly and Pratt, 1989) by which to monitor labour on behalf of absentee owners.

Many of these proposed uses of accounting (and CI) information fall well outside the normal expectations of economic rationality. Yet, there is evidence that these roles are real in practice (see, for example, Bower, 1970; Mintzberg, Raisinghani and Theoret, 1976).

What does this mean for CI decision-making? It is difficult to answer this question well: perhaps the best response is to note that CI decision-making is not as clear-cut as we might first imagine. It is influenced by a range of differing decision-making approaches and "rationalities", and the output from CI analyses may be used in a number of very different ways.

For example, the results of a CI project's NPV analysis may be used as an economic input to the decision, reflecting the project's

---

[2] Kelly and Pratt (1989) have elaborated on Chua's discussion of these "roles" and some of their thoughts are incorporated here.

financial viability. Alternatively, a positive NPV result may be seen as a political bargaining tool. A divisional manager who wants to secure organizational resources (and therefore political influence) for his own division might point to a positive NPV project as an example of the lucrative investment opportunities available to that division. Then, not only are the analysis results assisting the economic decision to go ahead with a viable project, they are also being used as ammunition in a resource bargaining situation which may produce a political advantage for the division manager. Where such a bargaining situation is looming, there may often be a temptation to *make* the NPV results look good, as a lack of attractive investment opportunities would reflect poorly on a division's future success. Which objective then takes precedence? This becomes a function of the organizational climate and of the individual decision-maker's preferences, and there may be no one right answer.

The main implication of this is that CI decision-making practice cannot be understood without considering the organizational and political contexts within which it occurs. CI decisions influence, and are influenced by, other aspects of organizational activity.

Let us now focus on two key aspects of organizational activity which have clear links with CI decision-making: performance evaluation and motivation, and strategic planning.

PERFORMANCE EVALUATION AND MOTIVATION

People whose task it is to make CI decisions often face a dilemma. A decision which appears "economically rational" may not always serve alternative rationalities which the decision-maker may be pursuing. Particularly, a decision-maker may perceive conflict between decisions which serve organizational goals and those which advance his or her own personal goals.

For CI decision-making we have seen that economically rational decisions are promoted by the use of NPV analyses, together with appropriate considerations of risk. The NPV approach requires that the decision-maker focuses on the long-term, uncertain cashflows from a CI project. The NPV method aims to maximize the value of the organization, and hence the wealth of the investors or owners.

However, it is difficult in practice to ensure that CI decision-makers will adopt this focus, unless they are somehow motivated to do so. Such motivation requires that the performance evaluation system rewards behaviour which promotes the economic goals of the organization. Failure to reward "economically rational" decisions may contribute to the theory–practice gap, where CI decision-making behaviour is observed which contradicts normative, theoretical expectations.

It is important to consider the potential causes of goal conflict, and ways in which it might be overcome so that CI decision-makers are better motivated to make decisions which are in the interests of the organization. There are several ways in which the organizational environment of CI decision-makers can create decision-making goal conflict.

Long-term v. short-term goals

Most organizations have both long-term and short-term goals. Since CI concerns the long-term commitment of resources, it follows that CI decision-making goals should have a long-term orientation. Indeed as already noted, the recommended NPV method for CI analysis has just such a long-term focus.

However, the difficulty lies in evaluating the "success" of CI decision-makers in meeting these long-term goals. A major difficulty lies in measuring the success of a long-term CI project. In assessing the success of the decision-maker, some measure of the project's success is implicitly required. It may be many years before the outcome of a CI is known, and even then it is difficult to ascertain the benefits which have accrued from the CI. How can anyone tell what *might* have happened if some other CI decision had been taken? Perhaps an alternative decision may have produced better or worse results than were actually achieved?

This problem creates difficulty in the evaluation of CI decision-makers. There is often a large time-lag between decision and outcome. It may be unfeasible to wait until the CI outcome is known before evaluating and rewarding the decision-maker. Indeed, the decision-maker responsible for an investment decision may have long since departed from the organization before a CI project is completed, or perhaps even started.

Since long-term goals are so difficult to evaluate, many organizations adopt shorter-term "surrogate" measures of CI success. However, improved linkages between performance measures and CI decisions have the potential to promote more effective CI decision-making. Indeed, Haka (1987, p. 45) supports this suggestion. She performed correlational analyses between firm-specific contingencies (such as performance measurement) and CI practice and found that "a [strong] relationship was found . . .

between the tendency of the firm to reward on the basis of long term performance and the effectiveness of DCFT [discounted cash flow techniques]." CI decision-makers should be encouraged to have long-term horizons, and the organizational reward structure should reflect this.

Accounting v. wealth maximization performance measures

Here we find one of the major practical difficulties of motivating and rewarding CI decision-makers. Short- to medium-term performance targets for which managers (including CI decision-makers) are commonly held accountable tend to be expressed in accounting terms. Often these are profit improvement, return on investment or earnings per share objectives which managers are expected to achieve. These objectives can often form the basis of remuneration packages which involve bonuses or target-linked promotion.

This creates a problem for long-term CI decision-making. As Emmanuel, Otley and Merchant (1990, p. 318) note:

> Discounted cash flow techniques are recommended to evaluate [CI] projects but the divisional manager's financial results may be evaluated on an accruals income basis. A fundamental concern is that managers will propose projects which improve short-term accounting profit for the division but which are second-best ones for the company.

This problem can be illustrated by way of an example.

EXAMPLE 7.1

CI decisions and performance measurement: goal incongruence

The manager of West Waste Disposal Ltd's recycling division has a component of her salary paid as a bonus, based on annual accounting rate of return (AROR) results. The company uses the "initial investment" method for determining AROR. At the moment, the recycling division's annual profit result is £40,000, and the historical initial outlays of all assets held by the division total £130,000.

The manager also has responsibility for CI expenditure in her division, for projects with an initial outlay of up to £30,000. She

is currently considering a CI project which has the following relevant characteristics:
- initial outlay = £20,000
- annual real net cashflow = +£4,000 p.a. (there are no non-cash items associated with this project)
- expected life = ten years
- real required rate of return = 10%

Calculating the project's NPV

NPV = −£20,000 + (+£4,000 × annuity factor: 10% for ten years)
$\quad$ = −£20,000 + (+£4,000 × 6.1446)
$\quad$ = +£4,578

So, the project should be accepted, as it has a positive NPV.

Calculating the project's effect on AROR

1. Existing AROR:
   = £40,000 ÷ £130,000
   = 30.8%
2. Revised AROR if the CI project is accepted:
   = (£40,000 + £4,000) ÷ (£130,000 + £20,000)
   = 29.3%

Therefore, although the CI project has a positive NPV, it will reduce the division's AROR results, thus reducing the manager's salary bonus. The manager is faced with a dilemma!

As demonstrated in Example 7.1, there is little incentive for CI decision-makers to support projects which have the best long-term benefit (as measured by NPV), if their own personal financial situation is penalized by an incongruent performance evaluation system.

These goal incongruence problems can be mitigated by supplementing (or replacing) accounting-based performance measures with some consideration of CI project performance. For example, actual cashflows from a CI project can be compared (via post audit) with *projected* cashflows which were put forward at the initiation of the project. Then, the decision-maker is free to make "economically rational" decisions based on NPV, without concern for accounting-based performance measures. Instead, the decision-maker becomes responsible for accurately assessing CI proposals, and for effective implementation of the project.

This approach, although potentially useful, still has practical shortcomings where post audit is unreliable, or where the CI decision-maker has little or no control over project implementation.

However, more appropriate variations are possible, which at least avoid clear personal goal conflict where a manager's remuneration is tied to some measure which is totally divorced from the DCF world of CI decisions.

Authority v. responsibility

A further difficulty in promoting economically rational CI decisions lies with the matching of authority and responsibility. If CI decision-makers are to be assessed by (and held responsible for) the outcomes of CI projects, they must have corresponding authority to effect that outcome.

Three problems arise here. First, CI decisions are rarely made by only one person. Usually, a project proposal must travel through a hierarchy of organizational decision-makers, usually requiring a group commitment, rather than a single person's recommendation. In fact, often the further along the commitment "chain" a CI proposal progresses, the less influence an individual decision-maker can exert. Acceptance of a CI proposal becomes almost a foregone conclusion, once sufficient organizational members have become involved with, and committed to, the decision. Singling out, and rewarding, the performance of any individual decision-maker in a CI project decision therefore may be almost impossible.

Further problems may arise in the project implementation and post audit phases. No matter how well a CI project is researched, analysed and considered, the decision-maker rarely has influence over the physical implementation of the project. Poor control in the implementation phase can ruin a potentially viable CI. Again, this creates problems for identifying results with decisions, and assessing the performance of the decision-makers.

Also, where project leaders who have a personal commitment to a CI project are providing post audit information, there may be a temptation to bias this information to make the project look good. If the responsibility for post audit information is creating a conflict of interest situation, appropriate performance evaluation methods can reduce the potential for misinformation. By considering the input and comments of other people involved in the CI project, the performance of the project leader can be more objectively assessed. Consequently, the incentive for the project leader to present incorrect post audit information is reduced, as there is a greater chance of being caught in the act of fudging the numbers!

Finally, political machinations in an organization may take away the real authority of a CI decision-maker. CI decisions may be swept along by a political agenda over which individual CI decision-makers have little control, and indeed of which they may not even be aware. Emmanuel, Otley and Merchant (1990, p. 324) refer to the work of an earlier researcher (Berg, 1965), who "observed that the capital budgeting process in the company he investigated was really a 'game' with the rules being defined by the measurement, control and reward schemes, the pressure for current profits and the administered profit goals".

"Game-playing" takes away clear linkages between good decision-making and successful outcomes. Decisions may become more important for their political contribution than for their economic value. Measuring whether a decision was "right" becomes difficult when the success criteria are political and nebulous. Therefore, the performance–reward linkage is broken. CI decision-makers may become demotivated if they make recommendations based on well-executed NPV analyses, only to have those recommendations overtaken by organizational game-playing.

All three of these difficulties blur the required nexus between authority and responsibility in CI decision-making. If an individual does not have authority to effect a CI outcome, then they cannot correctly be held responsible for the CI decision. Performance evaluation becomes problematic, and the lack of real authority may be demotivating for the decision-maker, thus acting against goal congruence.

Risk aversion

A CI decision-maker whose personal remuneration is tied to the success of CI projects may exhibit risk aversion. This can impact upon CI decisions by biasing individual decision-makers towards low-risk, low-return projects.

We know that, theoretically, a risky project is just as attractive as a less risky project, as long as the expected return is adequate to compensate for the level of risk. However, for a CI decision-maker, a safe, modest-return CI option may appear more attractive than a risky, high-return option. After all, the damage sustained for a bad result may be much more significant for a decision-maker's career (and remuneration) than the glory of an outstanding result. Opting for the high-risk CI option exposes the individual decision-maker – it's a big career gamble to take.

It can also be personally perilous for someone to make public a CI idea, if the performance evaluation environment is not tolerant of innovation and risk-taking. Often idea generation requires an element of "brain storming". Some of the ideas which emerge early in this process may seem weak or even outrageous, but they may lead to viable CI prospects once the idea has been further developed. It is important that people's contributions to idea development be recognized in performance evaluation and reward systems. If people are discouraged from presenting their ideas for fear of being ignored, or even humiliated, then good CI opportunities can be missed.

The "riskiness" problem in taking responsibility for CI decisions is accentuated where the decision-maker is evaluated by short-term, accounting measures. A CI project may be considered more risky if its cash outflows are more distant,[3] and so short-term accounting measures (e.g. annual contribution to profit) will put such a project in a bad light. Few CI decision-makers, knowing that they are personally evaluated by short-term accounting measures, will favour a project which is a slow starter. This creates goal conflict, as, in the long-term, such a project may be a good choice for the organization.

Performance evaluation and motivation: summary

Resolving conflict between personal and organizational objectives is a difficult task for the CI decision-maker. The level of goal conflict can be reduced if performance measurement systems take into account the specific problems of CI decision-making, i.e.:

- the long-term nature of CI projects
- the difficulty of assessing "wealth maximization" success using surrogate accounting measures
- the involvement of many organizational members in project decision-making and implementation
- the risk/return trade-off in evaluating CI proposals.

In order to foster CI decisions which are in the economic interests of the organization, there must be a recognition of the interrelationship between CI decision-making, motivation and performance appraisal. It is rarely sufficient to expect that all organizational members unswervingly pursue organizational economic goals. We know that there are many other equally

---

[3] Of course, the NPV approach, which uses a risk-adjusted discount rate, implicitly discounts distant cashflows more than it does near cashflows.

"rational" goals which people may value. The CI decision-making activities of an organization are therefore enhanced by a broad perspective and appreciation of how CI fits into the organizational environment.

STRATEGIC PLANNING AND DECISION-MAKING

Early case study work by Bower (1970) first began to recognize the strong links between CI decision-making and strategic planning and decision-making. Increasingly, authors refer to "strategic investment decision-making" when discussing CI type activities (see, for example, Butler *et al.*, 1991). To understand this relationship, it is important to identify the characteristics of "strategic decisions". Wilson and Chua (1988, p. 140) list seven basic characteristics of strategic decisions:[4]

1. they are concerned with the scope of an organization's activities, and hence with the definition of the organization's boundaries
2. they match the organization's activities with its environmental opportunities
3. they match an organization's activities with its resources
4. they have major resource implications
5. they are influenced by the values and expectations of those who determine the organization's strategy
6. they affect the organization's long-term direction
7. they are complex in nature.

All these characteristics of strategic decisions apply equally to our understanding of CI decisions. CI decisions are long-term, dictating major resource allocations which will affect the future direction and activities of the organization. They are complex decisions which must take account of the organization's environment, and they are often influenced by the values and expectations of those who have a hand in determining the organization's overall strategic direction.

It is clear that CI can be viewed as part of the strategic decision-making activity of an organization. Since CI decision-making is linked inextricably with the long-term strategic direction of an organization, it cannot be seen as a discrete, independent activity. Like other strategic decisions, CI decisions must be responsive to factors such as the firm's technology, goals and environment.

---

[4] Wilson and Chua's points have been condensed here, for simplicity.

These factors are often nebulous, uncertain and difficult to incorporate within quantitative decision models.

It is interesting to note a comment by Marsh *et al.* (1988, p. 20) about the relationship between strategic planning and CI decision-making. They noted that, in one firm where they studied CI practice, that:

> although the project we monitored was entirely consistent with, and apparently flowed from, the division's strategic plan, it would be equally true to say that the strategic plan was itself shaped by the foreshadowed existence of the project.

This illustrates again the familiar "chicken and egg" question regarding the order of the CI decision-making "process". Do CI decisions flow from the strategic plan as a natural manifestation of broader organizational goals? Normative CI models might suggest this to be so. But, there is evidence that the relationship between strategic planning and CI is a much more interactive, reflective one. CI is an integral part of strategic planning, which therefore occurs *alongside* strategic planning, rather than subsequent to it.

All this indicates that it is misleading (and potentially counter-productive) to focus only on the quantitative financial tools used in CI analysis. The strategic success of CI decision-making requires a much broader focus. As noted in Chapter 6, we have limited knowledge of just how strong the link between strategic planning and CI is in practice. However, it is becoming more apparent that the complex, organizational activity of strategy formulation cannot be separated from the CI activity. CI decision-making cannot be appropriately practised, or understood, outside the context of the organization, or apart from the people within the organization who determine strategy.

SUMMARY: A BEHAVIOURAL APPROACH TO CI DECISION-MAKING

In this chapter we have considered a broadened perspective of what drives CI decision-making practice. It has been noted that there is a "theory–practice gap" in our understanding of CI. Prescribed, "sophisticated" techniques designed to support CI decision-making are not necessarily used in practice in the way we might expect.

This chapter has suggested that this theory–practice gap is perhaps better understood as a "rationality perspective gap".

Normative CI theory is based on a single perspective of rational behaviour, derived from economics theory. However, recently authors have suggested that there are many alternative perspectives of rationality which may be equally important in the day-to-day decision-making of individuals within organizations. Social factors (relating to the expectations of "normal" behaviour within a socialized group of organizational members) and political factors (relating to the advancing of personal power and status) may well impinge on CI decision-making practice. It is not unreasonable to expect that observed behaviour which pursues multiple rationalities may not match expected behaviour based on a single rationality. Hence theory is mismatched with practice.

Along these lines, the uses to which accounting information is put are suggested to be many and varied. The financial output of NPV calculations are usually thought of as supporting the making of optimal economic decisions. However, this information may equally be employed in symbolic, ritualistic, political and retrospective rationalization roles. Financial information is a tool, used by decision-makers to support their particular pursuit of "rationality". CI analysis information is no different. It is not an answer in itself; it simply supports the efforts of decision-makers in arriving at their own (economic, social and political) answers.

When we look back at the traditional model of the CI decision-making process presented in Chapter 2, it is clear that such a model is overly simplistic. The ordered, mechanistic "process", from generating CI ideas to post auditing them for feedback purposes, is a product of an economic rationality perspective. Although strategic planning and personnel are seen as impacting on the CI process, they are also somehow *outside* the CI decision-making activity. The model has no iterative loops, no intervention of external or political factors in the process, and no recognition of the unprogrammed chaos which often characterizes decision-making practice.[5]

Can we model the CI decision-making activity more realistically? Probably not. The organizational context of CI decisions means that many facets of CI practice are contingent on the particular organization and its members. If a "universal" model of the CI decision-making activity *could* be presented, it might look something like Figure 7.1. A model like this is little help in explaining,

---

[5] March and Olsen (1976) discuss a "garbage can" descriptive model of decision-making, suggesting that people, problems and solutions often combine almost randomly, rather than being ordered in any way.

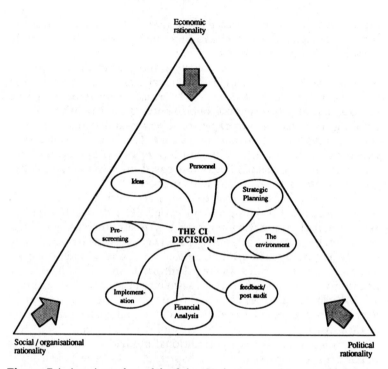

Figure 7.1 A universal model of the CI decision-making activity?

describing or understanding practice, and does little to direct theory development!

CONCLUSION

What the reader should take from this behavioural discussion of CI decision-making is a sense of perspective. The aim of this chapter is to provide balance; to add a pinch of people and "reality" to the abstract world of CI analysis theory.

If the reader is ever faced with the task of contributing to CI decisions, hopefully a faint memory of this discussion will help to make sense of the place of sophisticated financial analyses in a complex, human, organizational environment!

The next chapter presents a case study and discussion – a chance to bring together the quantitative and behavioural perspectives of CI decision-making in practice.

Problems

1. What are the assumptions of rational economic theory which have shaped traditional understanding of CI decision-making?

2. You overhear a senior manager say to her management accountant:

   You'll just have to take those numbers away and do them again. The boss really wants to go ahead with this plant expansion, and he's not going to appreciate me presenting him with a financial analysis which indicates a no-go decision!

   Discuss the way(s) in which accounting information is being used in this situation.

3. Suggest ways in which a performance evaluation system can incorporate the objectives of CI decision-making. Discuss approaches to, and problems of, measuring:
   (a) the "effectiveness" of CI decisions
   (b) the contribution of individual decision-makers to these decisions.

4. Discuss the role of effective post audit in the performance evaluation of CI decision-makers.

5. What are the characteristics of CI decision-making which make it a "strategic" type of activity?

6. What do you think might be the practical difficulties of incorporating a strategic focus within CI decision-making?

8

Illustrative Case Study: Capital Investment Decision-Making in Practice

INTRODUCTION

The case which follows challenges the reader to consider the complexity of CI decisions in practice. The case is presented in four sections:

- background of the organization
- the "formal" capital investment system
- the current CI proposal under consideration
- a discussion between four people involved in presenting and assessing this CI proposal.

The reader must undertake the kinds of financial analyses which could be used to evaluate the CI proposal in question, and also incorporate other information into a recommendation as to whether the proposed investment should be undertaken. The reader is also asked to consider the behavioural aspects of the decision-making process illustrated in this case.

144

Questions are provided as guidelines for considering the main elements of the case, and a discussion at the conclusion of this chapter highlights many of the issues which should be identified. However, the reader may infer much more from the information provided, and further avenues for exploration may emerge.

FOSTERS CONSTRUCTION LTD: ORGANIZATIONAL BACKGROUND

Fosters Construction Ltd (FCL) is a privately owned company with revenue of £20 million per annum, and 200 employees. The company has been operating for 24 years and is well established in the market-place. However, despite a national inflation rate of 4 per cent per annum over the last few years (which is expected to continue), a general economic downturn has seen FCL's nominal revenue reduce at a rate of about 3 per cent per annum.

The company's main activity is the construction of large industrial buildings. It also provides maintenance services, mainly for those buildings which it has constructed. FCL has a large investment in construction machinery, and has always kept up with the latest technology in the industry. The company has concentrated on developing a corporate image as an innovative, technologically advanced construction firm, and many of the managers of FCL consider that this corporate image has been a major factor in securing large, competitive contracts in the past.

FCL is subject to corporation tax at 35 per cent, payable twelve months after year end, and a system of 25 per cent writing down allowance on capital assets.

FCL's FORMAL CAPITAL INVESTMENT SYSTEM

As investment in construction equipment is central to the operations of FCL, the organization has, over many years, developed a detailed system by which capital investment proposals are considered. The summary sheet below is taken from the firm's capital investment procedures manual, and outlines the formal process for capital investment decision-making within FCL.

FOSTERS CONSTRUCTION LTD.
CAPITAL INVESTMENT PROCEDURES –
SUMMARY

Capital investment (CI) is defined as "any major expenditure on purchasing, constructing or upgrading capital assets, the benefits from which will accrue over several years".

1. In early January of each year the CI budget is determined. The total amount of available funds for CI expenditure is determined by the directors, based on what they consider the company can afford.

2. Later that month, divisional managers meet to discuss forthcoming CI requirements, and the budget is allocated across divisions. Managers must present their proposed CI requirements under the following three headings:
   (i) essential replacement of existing assets (Class 1)
   (ii) strategic expansion (Class 2)
   (iii) safety and regulatory expenditure (Class 3)
The final allocation across divisions is a decision taken jointly by the CEO and the director of CI.

3. Throughout the year, access to funds for investment requires the submission of a standard form CI/12 – Capital Expenditure Application. The information normally required with such a submission includes:
   (i) a description of the proposed investment
   (ii) motivation for the investment, i.e. what will the investment achieve for the company
   (iii) financial projections of the cost of the investment
   (iv) projected future financial benefits of the investment
   (v) key success indicators for the investment (used for assessing the riskiness of the project and for subsequent post audit)
   (vi) a projected time-scale for completion of the investment
However, proposed Class 3 projects may dispense with items (iv) and (v), and those in Class 1 may dispense with items (ii), (iv) and (v).

4. The CI/12 form is assessed by the director of CI, who has the following options:
   (i) accept the proposal and forward it to the CEO for financing approval
   (ii) refer the proposal back for further refinement

(iii) reject the proposal

CI proposals will be assessed with regard to the net present value (NPV) and payback period (PP) of the proposed project, although Class 1 projects will be considered as "cost minimization exercises", since there is already an accepted need to continue with current operations and assets, and Class 3 projects are not required to meet financial criteria.

5. All CI projects are assessed within a ten-year planning horizon, i.e. investment effects beyond this ten-year horizon are considered uncertain, and are ignored.

6. If approved, a CI proposal is then allocated funds from the annual budget. A project supervisor is then assigned, and this person is responsible for the implementation and reporting of the CI project.

7. In due course, some selected CI projects will be subject to post audit by the director of CI.

THE CURRENT CI DECISION: PURCHASE OF A REPLACEMENT CRANE

The construction site manager (CSM) has recently submitted a CI/12 application for the purchase of a new crane. This new asset would replace an existing crane which is ten years old, and which requires major maintenance in order to meet required safety standards. The CSM had indicated in the January budget-setting round that the firm would need to spend money on maintaining the old crane, but had not at that stage been aware of any replacement options. It had previously been expected that the existing crane would see out its remaining useful life, to be replaced by a more modern crane in five years' time.

The CSM's proposal is to purchase a modern crane (the Auto-Lift II, or "AL II"). The AL II is technologically more advanced than the firm's existing crane, and is able to lift much larger loads. The new crane would cost £345,000, which is considerably more than the original £195,000 cost of the existing crane.

The CSM consulted with the site accountants, and put forward the following information in the CI/12 application:

1. Description: purchase of an AL II crane to replace an existing crane which is in need of major maintenance.

2. Cost projections: purchase price = £345,000; annual running costs = £60,000. It is expected that the AL II crane would have a £30,000 scrap value at the end of its useful life in ten years' time.
3. Projected time-scale: available for purchase from Allied Importers Ltd in one month's time. Purchase price payable on 31 March – the last day of FCL's financial year for taxation purposes.

The site accountants and the CSM had agreed that no further information was necessary, as the CI proposal qualified as a "replacement of existing asset" Class 1 investment.

The CSM's CI/12 application has now been considered by the director of CI, who feels uneasy about recommending the AL II crane purchase for funding approval. The director of CI has called a meeting of concerned parties to discuss the CI application.

THE MEETING PARTICIPANTS

The following people are present at the meeting to discuss the AL II purchase proposal:

Sonya Carson (SC) Director of CI. Sonya is new to this position, and is familiarizing herself with the technical nature of the firm's operations. She has an undergraduate economics degree and is considered competent, if perhaps a little over-ambitious. However, many longer-serving organizational members doubt Sonya's ability to make good decisions regarding investment in an industry about which she currently knows little. For this reason, her appointment to the position of director of CI was controversial.

Julian Done (JD) Construction site manager. Julian has worked in the construction industry for 15 years, progressing through the ranks to become CSM two years ago. He is considered to be competent in his job, but is perceived as uncompromising and confrontational. Julian has no time for "the head office bosses", and his outspoken manner at meetings has often met with disapproval from the CEO.

Franc Silvero (FS) CEO of Foster's Construction Ltd. Franc came to FCL seven years ago when the construction industry was in a boom period. He received much accolade for record sales levels when he first joined the firm as contracts director, and so has continued to implement the policies which had met with success in the past. Franc is now perceived as conservative, and often resists movement towards new areas of business operations. He has a construction background, and sometimes feels uncomfortable with his new managerial role as CEO.

Henry Morton (HM) Engineering manager. Henry has an engineering degree and has worked in the trade for eight years, joining FCL three years ago. Henry is often called on to give advice on the technical and operating implications of capital asset purchases, as well as their probable maintenance costs. Henry keeps up-to-date on innovation and new technology in the construction industry, and his opinion is well respected. However, Henry has in the past been frustrated in several attempts to introduce advanced technology into FCL's construction equipment, and blames this on the conservative approach of Franc Silvero.

THE MEETING

The meeting called by Sonya turned out to be lengthy and lively. There was considerable debate, and the following excerpt reflects the main comments raised by the participants.

> **SC**: Look Julian, there just isn't enough information here. I have to be able to work out the new crane's NPV and payback period. In the past, if projects haven't had a positive NPV at a required rate of return of 26 per cent, and paid back within five years, then they haven't been approved. Do we know anything about the financial benefits which the AL II might produce? What advantage is there in buying this thing now? Couldn't we just let our old crane run its course and consider our options once it reaches the end of its useful life in a few years' time?

> **FS**: Yes, I think we need to look more closely at the details here. Julian, what do you think the outlook is if we stay with the old crane?

> **JD**: The old crane really needs some maintenance work done on it, to bring it up to safety standards. If we spent about £40,000 on maintenance straight away it should be OK until it goes out of commission in five years' time.

> **FS**: What does it cost us to run the old crane?

> **JD**: Running costs are around £40,000 per annum. Plus, the crane's

getting unreliable. I reckon there's about a 50 per cent chance that it will break down at some time during the year. If it does we lose three days' productivity on a job at a cost of around £15,000, not to mention the cost of fixing it, which was £10,000 last time. Even once it's fixed there's still a 50 per cent chance it could break down again within the next twelve months.

FS: OK. What if we go for the AL II?

JD: The running costs would be a bit higher, as it's a finely tuned machine and needs regular maintenance. I reckon we're looking at about £60,000 a year, judging by the recommended service programme. But, at least it's not likely to break down. Also, I'm sure the AL II would improve our chances of winning contracts – it's faster and it will help keep costs down. Take for example that Storex contract we missed out on last month. The kind of cost savings we could get with the AL II could have won us that bid, and jobs like that are worth around £40,000 in pre-tax profit to FCL. We could pick up a couple more like that one each year – maybe more.

FS: How would you rate the chances of picking up more work with the AL II?

JD: Well, probably about a 60 per cent chance that we'd get another two like the Storex job each year, and perhaps about a 20 per cent chance of doubling that. It's hard to say really, but the customers out there are feeling the pinch – we've got to watch our cost competitiveness if we want to stay in the game.

HM: That's a key point here, I think. We've got to take a long-term view. The way I read it, these AL II cranes will take over the market in the next two years, and by the time we came to replace our old crane five years from now, we'd be looking at buying an AL II anyway. The question is, do we get in on the new technology now, or in five years' time?

We really can't assume that the status quo will continue if we don't go for the AL II now. We're looking at a fall in price competitiveness, company image and profits if we don't move with the times. If we *do* go with the AL II now, we've got an edge over our competitors. Even then, we wouldn't want to hang on to the AL II for more than ten years – we need to keep upgrading to keep ahead of the game.

JD: I can't see what the problem is with these numbers Sonya has to crunch. It's only an asset replacement, and I've given you all of the information the manual says you need. Besides, I told everyone in January that we'd need to spend some money on the crane, so we all knew this was coming.

FS: That's true, Julian, but we're talking £345,000 now, whereas we only expected to spend £40,000 on maintenance. I'm not at all sure that we want to get into experimental technology anyway, it seems pretty risky. What's wrong with maintaining the old crane, as planned? It's still got five years left in it, and they're pretty hard to sell second-hand. It's in our books at £10,981 after accumulated WDAs. We'd probably only get about £20,000 for it if we went to sell it, which isn't much more than the £5,000 scrap value we'd get for it in five years' time.

SC: Julian, perhaps you, Henry and I can sit down and draw up the figures, including the cost and benefit information you've mentioned today. Then I can run the numbers and see if it meets our investment criteria.

There's just a couple of things that bother me, though. It doesn't seem right to use the same required rate of return for every project. We should be using different rates for different types of projects. I've been playing around with a few numbers, and it seems to me that 26 per cent is too high. It might be OK for risky projects that are something new to us, but here we're talking about a crane. That's run-of-the-mill stuff for FCL, and it seems to me that a 21 per cent nominal required return would be more appropriate.

Also, looking at past records of CI analyses, it looks like the 26 per cent rate has been used as a *real* discount rate, when it is actually calculated to represent a nominal rate. We really need to do some inflation adjustments to the rates we're using.

JD: This is all gobbledegook to me. Perhaps *that's* the problem here – we're so tied up in the numbers that we can't see a good investment when it hits us in the face!

FS: We have to be sure that any investment is financially viable, Julian. Sonya, why don't you run the numbers both ways: the way we have in the past, and again using a rate you think is appropriate. I'd be interested in seeing what difference it makes, although there's never been a shortage of projects in the past that have made the 26 per cent grade. I hope you wouldn't be cutting it too fine using a rate like 21 per cent. It doesn't seem to leave much margin for error if our project estimates turn out to be wrong.

SC: I'll run the numbers, but the best way of dealing with margins for error is by getting things right in the first place. There's still a lot of uncertainty in this project. All we've got so far are "feelings" and estimates – do you think we can firm up those figures at all?

JD: No. There just isn't any other information. Look, I've been in this industry since before you finished school – I've learnt enought to know what's what. I can tell you now that sooner or later we'll need a new crane to be able to do our jobs, and doing our jobs is what makes money for this company!

FS: OK, Julian, no one's doubting your judgement. Sonya, how about doing what you suggested, and sitting down with Henry and Julian. They should be able to give you the technical information, and you can work through the numbers. I'd like to see the IRR too – I've never been able to understand why we don't calculate IRR. I know a lot of other firms that do.

HM: Maybe we could think about changing the CI procedures manual too. That way, the technical people will know exactly what information the director of CI needs, and things can be settled faster.

SC: Fine, that's a good idea. Look, I know we haven't resolved this, but thanks for coming to this meeting. Perhaps we can all get together again in a week's time to make a decision.

DISCUSSION QUESTIONS

1. Present the financial analyses required by FCL's CI procedures manual, as they have traditionally been calculated. Explain any assumptions you make. According to FCL's usual decision criteria, would the AL II be purchased now?

2. Explain to JD the difference between real and nominal RRRs, as mentioned by SC. What adjustment to SC's suggested RRR would be needed in order to match the discount rate with the cashflows used?

3. Re-calculate the NPV of the AL II purchase proposal, using what Sonya Carson would consider to be an appropriate RRR. Do these revised NPV results suggest that the AL II should be purchased?

4. In the light of your calculations for the AL II purchase proposal, what would be your response to FS's comment that the IRR of projects should be calculated?

5. What do you think might be the key variables in the AL II investment which will affect its viability? How might you consider these uncertain variables in better assessing the proposal?

6. What further information would be useful in analysing the AL II proposal?
7. Identify any problems that you see regarding the following:
   (a) the current CI procedures manual (as outlined in the summary)
   (b) communication and consultation between the people involved in, and affected by, the CI decision.
8. Do you consider that it would be wise to conduct a post audit if this asset were purchased, to see if it is achieving the expected benefits? If so, how might you use the findings of such a post audit?
9. Suggest changes to FCL's CI procedures which might improve future CI decision-making.

DISCUSSION

There are many issues which may arise from this case study. Some financial analyses and other concerns are presented here as starting points for considering readers' responses.

Financial analyses

The tables which follow present:

1. A summary of the WDA taxation effects under each of the two options available to FCL (purchasing the AL II immediately, or deferring the AL II purchase until the existing crane has completed its useful life in five years' time).
2. The cashflows relevant to each option.
3. A summary of differential cashflows, together with the calculations of the NPV and PP of the "purchase AL II now" option, as required by the CI procedures manual.

Writing down allowance taxation effects

The 25 per cent writing down allowance (WDA) on capital assets has implications for taxation cashflows. The amount of the taxation effect can be found by multiplying the write down amount by the tax rate (35 per cent). The timing of this cashflow depends upon the time at which the capital asset was purchased. The information in the case reveals that both the existing crane and the proposed AL II crane start their lives on the last day of the financial/taxation year. Hence, the WDA taxation effects occur one year after the write down occurs.

Table 8.1 shows the taxation cashflow effects of the WDAs allowable on both the old crane and the proposed AL II. Readers may achieve differing results, depending on how assumptions about residual values and unequal asset lives are treated. However, the calculations presented here reflect one possible approach, and will form the basis for the financial analyses presented later.

Notes to Table 8.1

1. The current book value of the existing ten-year-old crane (as stated by FS). This can also be derived by subtracting ten years' worth of WDA from the initial purchase price (£195,000) of the existing crane.
2. The current purchase price of the AL II. Also note that, if the AL II is purchased, there will be a tax effect from the balancing charge when the old crane is sold:
   - book value = £10,981; expected selling price = £20,000
   - gain on sale = (£20,000 − £10,981) = £9,019
   - balancing charge (tax payable) = (£9,019 × 0.35) = £3,157, payable in year 1. This will be noted later, in the NPV and PP calculations.
3. In five years from now, the old crane would be scrapped:
   - book value = £2,606; expected scrap value = £5,000
   - gain on sale = (£5,000 − £2,606) = £2,394
   - balancing charge (tax payable) = (£2,394 × 0.35) = £838, payable in year 6.
4. In the same year that the old crane is scrapped (i.e. year 5) the AL II replacement would be purchased. Hence, the first WDA on the replacement AL II also occurs in year 5, the taxation effect of which accrues in year 6.
5. Since FCL works to a ten-year planning horizon, only WDA effects up to year 10 are considered. (Some readers may choose to omit cashflows that occur in year 11 for the same reason.) Under the "retain the old crane" option, the AL II replacement purchased in year 5 would still have five years' life remaining at the end of the ten-year planning horizon.

   This presents a variation of an "unequal lives" comparison problem. This can be tackled using the equivalent annual cashflow approach, or by estimating a salvage value for the option which has some remaining life at the end of the ten-year planning horizon (the AL II). The second approach will be adopted here for illustrative purposes.

Table 8.1 WDA tax effects under each option: retain old crane or purchase AL II immediately

Time of write-down	Opening value (£) Old crane	AL II	Amount (£) of 25% WDA Old crane	AL II	35% tax effect (£) & timing Old crane	Yr	AL II	Yr
now	(1) **10,981**	(2) **345,000**	2,745	86,250	961	1	30,188	1
1st yr	8,236	258,750	2,059	64,688	721	2	22,641	2
2nd yr	6,177	194,062	1,544	48,516	540	3	16,981	3
3rd yr	4,633	145,546	1,158	36,387	405	4	12,735	4
4th yr	3,475	109,159	869	27,290	304	5	9,551	5
5th yr	2,606	81,869	(3) **−2,394**	20,467	−838	6	7,163	6
	(4) **345,000**	–	86,250	–	30,188	6	–	–
6th yr	258,750	61,402	64,688	15,350	22,641	7	5,372	7
7th yr	194,062	46,052	48,516	11,513	16,981	8	4,030	8
8th yr	145,546	34,539	36,387	8,635	12,735	9	3,022	9
9th yr	109,159	25,904	27,290	6,476	9,551	10	2,267	10
10th yr	81,869	19,428	(5) **−44,131**	(6) **−10,572**	−15,446	11	−3,700	11

Therefore, it is necessary to estimate the salvage value (s.v.) of the AL II option, as though it discontinues in year 10. There are many ways in which this salvage value could be estimated, and the analysis is fairly insensitive to the estimate used, as the cashflow is distant. Here it has been assumed that the five-year-old AL II would retain the same percentage of its book value (b.v.) as does the ten-year-old AL II. That is:

five-year-old AL II s.v.
    = (ten-year-old AL II s.v. ÷ ten-year-old AL II b.v.)
    ×five-year-old AL II b.v.
So: estimated year 10 AL II s.v.
    = (£30,000 ÷ £19,428) × £81,869
    = £126,000 (to the nearest £1,000)

Hence, on discontinuing this asset, it is assumed to sell for £126,000 and so:
- book value = £81,869; expected scrap value = £126,000
- gain on sale = (£126,000 − £81,869) = £44,131
- balancing charge (tax payable) = (£44,131 × 0.35) = £15,446, payable in year 11.
6. The AL II, if purchased now, would be at the end of its useful life in ten years' time. Therefore, it will be sold for its expected scrap value of £30,000 and so:
    - book value = £19,428; expected scrap value = £30,000
    - gain on sale = (£30,000 − £19,428) = £10,572
    - balancing charge (tax payable) = (£10,572 × 0.35) = £3,700, payable in year 11.

The cashflows relevant to each option

The WDA taxation effect is just one type of cashflow which is relevant to the capital investment decision facing FCL. Summaries of all known cashflow effects arising from each option (buy the AL II now, or defer purchase for five years) are presented in Tables 8.2 and 8.3, together with relevant assumptions and calculations.

Notes to Table 8.2

1. The cashflows presented for both the immediate and deferred AL II purchase options include only those items directly relevant to each option – i.e. current revenues and expenditures

Table 8.2 Cashflows associated with the immediate AL II purchase option

Cashflow (1)	Time 0	Yr 1	Yr 2	Yr 3	Yr 4	Yr 5	Yr 6	Yr 7	Yr 8	Yr 9	Yr 10	Yr 11
Purchase Price	−345,000											
Scrap old crane (tax in WDA)	+20,000											
Scrap AL II in year 10 (tax in WDA)											+30,000	
WDA/tax effects (35%)		+30,188	+22,641	+16,981	+12,735	+9,551	+7,163	+5,372	+4,030	+3,022	+2,267	−3,700
Running expenses		−60,000	−60,000	−60,000	−60,000	−60,000	−60,000	−60,000	−60,000	−60,000	−60,000	
−tax break on running expenses (35%)			+21,000	+21,000	+21,000	+21,000	+21,000	+21,000	+21,000	+21,000	+21,000	+21,000
New contracts won (2)		+80,000	+80,000	+80,000	+80,000	+80,000						
−tax on new contract revenue (35%)			−28,000	−28,000	−28,000	−28,000	−28,000					
Annual cashflows	−325,000	+50,188	+35,641	+29,981	+25,735	+22,551	−59,837	−33,628	−34,970	−35,978	−6,733	+17,300

Table 8.3 Cashflows associated with the option to defer purchase of the AL II

Cashflow	Time 0	Yr 1	Yr 2	Yr 3	Yr 4	Yr 5	Yr 6	Yr 7	Yr 8	Yr 9	Yr 10	Yr 11
Maintenance expense on old crane –tax break (35%)	–40,000	+14,000										
Scrap old crane in year 5 (tax in WDA)						+5,000						
Buy AL II in yr 5						–345,000						
Scrap AL II yr 10 (1) (tax in WDA)											+126,000	
WDA/tax effects (35%)		+961	+721	+540	+405	+304	(2) –838					
							+30,188	+22,641	+16,981	+12,735	+9,551	–15,446
Running expenses		–40,000	–40,000	–40,000	–40,000	–40,000	–40,000	–40,000	–40,000	–40,000	–40,000	
–tax break (35%)			+14,000	+14,000	+14,000	+14,000	+14,000	+14,000	+14,000	+14,000	+14,000	+14,000
Possibility of breakdown (3)		–12,500	–12,500	–12,500	–12,500	–12,500						
–tax break (35%)			+4,375	+4,375	+4,375	+4,375	+4,375					
Annual cashflows	–40,000	–37,539	–33,404	–33,585	–33,720	–373,821	+7,725	–3,359	–9,019	–13,265	+109,551	–1,446

which remain constant no matter which option is pursued, are omitted from the analysis.

2. There is a 60 per cent chance of gaining extra pre-tax profit of (2 × £40,000), and a 20 per cent chance of gaining (4 × £40,000). The expected value of new contracts is therefore (0.6 × £80,000) + (0.2 × £160,000) = £80,000. This cashflow is relevant for only the next five years, as beyond that FCL will be operating an AL II regardless of the current decision.

Notes to Table 8.3

1. Assumed scrap value of the five-year-old AL II in year 10, as used in the WDA calculations.
2. In Year 5, two depreciation effects occur: the scrapping of the old crane creates a balancing charge of −838, and the WDAs on the AL II purchased in year 5 commence.
3. If the old crane is retained for five more years, there is a continuing possibility of breakdown over these five years. Each breakdown is expected to cost £25,000 (£15,000 lost productivity + £10,000 repairs). As there is an estimated 50 per cent chance per annum of breakdown, the expected value of breakdowns is (0.50 × £25,000) or £12,500 p.a. There will also be a reduction in tax associated with the breakdown cost.

Differential cashflows and NPV and PP calculations

In order to calculate the NPV and PP of the decision to purchase the AL II crane immediately, differential cashflows must be derived. Table 8.4 shows the differential cashflows (obtained by subtracting the "defer option" cashflows from those of the "purchase immediately" option) together with NPV calculations.

NPV calculations The first set of NPV calculations shown in Table 8.4 uses the 26 per cent RRR criteria traditionally employed by FCL, to discount the *real* cashflows relevant to the investment decision. That is, the 26 per cent RRR is treated as a *real* RRR. The result is a negative NPV (−£31,561), suggesting that the AL II crane would not be purchased immediately if a 26 per cent RRR was imposed.

Without any information on market returns, the use of CAPM to assist in computing an appropriate RRR is ruled out. The next-best option is to use an RRR which is appropriate for the "risk class" of the CI, as is suggested by SC. However, since the AL II

Table 8.4 Differential cashflow analysis and NPVs using 26 per cent and 16 per cent discount rate

	Time 0	Yr 1	Yr 2	Yr 3	Yr 4	Yr 5	Yr 6	Yr 7	Yr 8	Yr 9	Yr 10	Yr 11
Purchase AL II now	-325,000	+50,188	+35,641	+29,981	+25,735	+22,551	-59,837	-33,628	-34,970	-35,978	-6,733	+17,300
Defer AL II purchase	-40,000	-37,539	-33,404	-33,585	-33,720	-373,821	+7,725	-3,359	-9,019	-13,265	+109,551	-1,446
Difference	-285,000	+87,727	+69,045	+63,566	+59,455	+396,372	-67,562	-30,269	-25,951	-22,713	-116,284	+18,746
Discount factor (26%)	1	.7937	.6299	.4999	.3968	.3149	.2499	.1983	.1574	.1249	.0992	.0787
Present value	-285,000	+69,629	+43,491	+31,777	+23,592	+124,818	-16,884	-6,002	-4,085	-2,837	-11,535	+1,475
NPV (26%) =	-£31,561											
Discount factor (16%)	1	.8621	.7432	.6407	.5523	.4761	.4104	.3538	.3050	.2629	.2267	.1954
Present value	-285,000	+75,629	+51,314	+40,727	+32,837	+188,713	-27,727	-10,709	-7,915	-5,971	-26,362	+3,663
NPV (16%) =	+£29,199											

represents new technology, SC is perhaps under-estimating the riskiness of the project relative to FCL's normal operations. However, without further information, the 21 per cent nominal RRR suggested by SC gives us the best estimate of an appropriate RRR.

Discussion question 2 asks for an explanation of the difference between real and nominal RRRs. Clearly, there has been some past confusion on this issue, with nominal rates being used to discount real cashflows. This error would lead to overly harsh discounting, and would make CI projects appear less attractive.

In this case no information is given about specific inflation indices for differing cost and revenue items. Therefore, it is not possible to adjust future cashflows to their nominal value. So, it is important that a real RRR be used to correctly discount the real cashflows. The 21 per cent nominal rate must be adjusted for general inflation (4 per cent):

$$(1 + \text{real RRR}) = (1 + \text{nominal RRR}) \div (1 + \text{inflation rate})$$
so: $(1 + \text{real RRR}) = (1 + 0.21) \div (1 + 0.04)$
so: $(1 + \text{real RRR}) = (1.163)$
$\text{Real RRR} = 16\%$ (rounded)

The *real* cashflows relating to the investment decision are then discounted by this inflation-adjusted RRR of 16 per cent.

It is interesting to explore some of the comments made by the decision-makers in the case, regarding the required rate of return. FS's argument that 21 per cent is too "risky" to use as an investment criterion is misguided. It is better to use realistic RRR criteria than to build in distorting "safety margins". The risk that the project may not achieve this RRR is better dealt with via sensitivity analysis.

FS has also noted that "there's never been a shortage of projects in the past that have made the 26 per cent grade". This may reflect an abundance of high-return investment opportunities available to FCL. Yet, this provides no justification for rejecting projects which meet a realistic RRR target, yet do not achieve a 26 per cent RRR. (Although the capital rationing situation faced, or self-imposed, by FCL may impact on the ranking and "cut-off point" of acceptable projects.) Alternatively, the success of many projects in meeting the 26 per cent requirement may reflect a tendency of project initiators to "pad" figures so that a known RRR requirement can be met. If this is occurring, the use of an artificially high RRR further promotes unrealistic cashflow projections, and reduces the reliability of ensuing analyses.

Either way, the use of a 16 per cent real RRR for NPV analyses provides better guidance to FCL's capital investment decision-makers. In this case, staying with the 26 per cent traditional RRR may result in the rejection of a viable investment opportunity.

Payback period Using the differential annual cashflows, the payback period for the immediate AL II purchase option is marginally greater than four years. If we can assume that the cashflows accrue evenly throughout the year, then the payback period is 4.01 years. Therefore, the immediate purchase of the AL II option would meet FCL's five years PP requirement.

Whether or not this PP result would influence the decision to be taken by FCL (especially in the light of the negative NPV result at the 26 per cent RRR), depends upon the relative weighting given to each analysis in making the decision. However, this does illustrate the conflicting results which differing analysis techniques can produce, and the danger of relying upon unsophisticated methods such as PP.

Should IRR be calculated?

There is little to be gained by calculating IRR. NPV is a superior technique which provides comprehensive and appropriate financial analyses to assist decision-making.

In the case of the AL II purchase proposal, IRR would have particular difficulties. The sign of the differential cashflows associated with the immediate AL II purchase changes from being positive (years 1 to 5), to negative (years 6 to 10) and back to positive (year 11). This creates the difficulty of "multiple root solutions" where the IRR analysis technique is employed. In fact, the AL II purchase option has IRR solutions at −84%, −17% and +20% discount rates. Such varying results would provide little guidance to a CI decision-maker.

The "other firms" to which FS refers may find the IRR approach attractive because it expresses a financial result as a percentage. This may appear to remove the need to establish an RRR criterion. However, IRR results must be compared with some RRR benchmark, and so the difficult issue of determining an appropriate RRR cannot be avoided. Overall, there is little to gain from FCL computing IRR as part of the CI financial analysis.

Key variables

It is always difficult to identify "key variables", without a good knowledge of the industry. However, the following factors appear to be significant:

- the expected useful life of the AL II (especially if technology is rapidly advancing and obsolescence may be a concern)
- the extent to which the AL II will affect the cost of fulfilling contracts, and the number of bids which could be won
- the running and maintenance costs of the AL II
- any possible changes to the purchase price of the AL II
- the date of payment for the AL II. If payment is delayed by only one day, it will push back the cashflows associated with WDAs by one year
- the realizable value of the old crane and likely salvage value of the AL II when it is five or ten years old
- the discount rate to be used in establishing the NPV of the proposal. It may be appropriate to conduct sensitivity analysis with respect to the discount rate. The expectation of 4 per cent inflation may also be incorrect
- the probability of the old crane breaking down, and associated costs
- the effect of FCL's crane technology on their market image and competitive advantage. This is difficult to quantify, but even using a 26 per cent RRR (NPV = −31,561) FCL may decide to undertake the AL II purchase in order to maintain competitive advantage, and to avoid further worsening of the company's operating results.

Probably the best way to deal with these uncertainties is to perform sensitivity analysis, recalculating the NPV of the AL II purchase for "optimistic" and "pessimistic" outcomes of each key variable. If any variable appears particularly critical to the viability of the AL II purchase, it may be worth FCL incurring some cost in obtaining better information about that variable, so that major potential causes of project failure are eliminated.

Additional information required

A number of points are listed here. Readers may be able to add to this list.

- Are there any crane replacement options which might be alternatives to the AL II purchase, either now or in five years' time? The viability of the AL II cannot be assessed without information about other options.
- Has JD obtained quotes from more than one supplier of the

AL II crane? Perhaps the £345,000 purchase price could be lowered by shopping around.

- Are exchange rate fluctuations likely to affect the import and purchase price of the AL II over the next month?
- ·What (if any) service support, warranties etc. come with the AL II? This will affect the expense which FCL might incur in maintaining the crane over the next few years. Are FCL's engineers able to maintain the technologically advanced AL II, or will retraining or contract maintenance be required?
- What anticipated time savings will the new asset bring about? This will impact on both the cost of completing normal construction contracts, and the number of additional contract bids which FCL is likely to win.
- Are there any hidden costs of purchasing the AL II? For example, will the current operator continue, or will retraining or a more skilled employee be required?
- Will any increase in working capital (e.g. construction materials) be required as a result of the AL II's increased work capacity?
- Strategic planning information may help to establish the extent to which FCL's future business is likely to decline if they continue with the existing crane. As FS noted, it may be misleading for FCL to assume that the status quo will continue if they do not keep up with technological advances in the industry. FCL must consider its strategic goals in considering an asset purchase which will take the firm into a new area of construction technology.

Problems

The CI manual

- Limited information requirements for replacement and safety/regulatory projects. In this case the information required is insufficient. How do they classify "replacement"? The AL II project may also be considered a "strategic" investment (Class 2), or a "safety" investment (Class 3) as it both advances the technological base of the organization and contributes to maintaining safety standards which the old crane currently fails to meet.
- The way in which the annual CI budget is set appears to be *ad hoc*. Also, budget determination takes no account of profitable investment opportunities which may arise. The meeting of divisional managers (where forthcoming CI requirements are

discussed) should take place *before* the CI budget is set. The budget-setting exercise, while restricted by available financing, should retain flexibility, allowing viable investment opportunities to be exploited.

- There seems to be some perception (e.g. by JD) that once a CI need has been approved in principle in the January budget, that there is less need to demonstrate its financial viability. This creates a danger of later, unexpected project opportunities being judged by different criteria, and perhaps disadvantaged.
- There is no direction given as to how "project supervisors" are to be selected. There may be a problem where the supervisor is also the project initiator, as that person may have a vested interest in ensuring that the project appears profitable. If that person is also responsible for providing information for post audit, evaluation may be biased. Independent post audit is usually best.
- How are those projects which are to be post audited selected? No guidelines are provided.
- It appears that CI decisions are at the final discretion of the director of CI. It may be useful to include higher authorization levels, wider personnel involvement in decision-making, and possibly rights of appeal against decisions taken by the director of CI.

Communication and consultation

- There is no explicit provision for consultation in completing CI/12 application forms. Perhaps the earlier involvement of people with expertise, such as HM, would help to arrange details of the project. Regular, scheduled meetings may be better than *ad hoc* consultations such as this one.
- The engineering manager apparently has no say in the allocation of the annual CI budget across divisions. His expertise and awareness of changing technology could be a useful input to budget allocation decisions.
- There appears to be a perception of alienation between the "decision-makers" (SC and FS) and the people who work with the capital assets (e.g. JD). SC's role as director of CI should be better communicated to the people with whom she must work. Similarly, SC could be more proactive in seeking information from people with technical expertise *before* a proposal reaches the formal assessment stage.
- In the case of the AL II decision, there did not appear to be any consultation with employees who must work with the

machine to be purchased. They may provide useful insights from their day-to-day experience with the existing crane.

Post audit

The decision whether or not to post audit a CI project depends upon the perceived costs and benefits of doing so. The costs primarily relate to necessary information systems, and the time of both those people who provide information and those people who assess the project. FCL must judge whether the benefits of post audit justify these costs in the case of the AL II purchase. The following factors may be relevant:

- Post audit may provide information for the improvement of future decisions. This AL II purchase decision is clearly problematic, and so any lessons learnt from the outcome may be valuable. However, it is not clear how well findings from a post audit of the AL II purchase would transfer to other CI decisions faced by FCL. If this asset purchase is out of the ordinary, the value of post audit may be lessened.
- Care is needed in assigning the project supervisor, who will be responsible for furnishing the information required for post audit. This person should be familiar with the project and technically competent, but not so close to the project that there is potential for bias (HM would seem a good choice, in the case of the AL II).
- The AL II purchase appears to be a sizeable investment, which may itself warrant some accountability for the use of FCL's funds, through post audit.
- Since the AL II is "strategic", in that it involves new technology, post audit may be useful in establishing the benefits which can arise from this type of investment.
- Post audit of CIs can be useful in assessing the performance of those people involved in CI decision-making and project implementation. The extent to which post audit can assist performance appraisal depends on how well the investment's outcome can be related to the decisions and actions of individuals.
- The measurability of the AL II's costs and benefits will influence the usefulness of post audit. It may be difficult to separate out those operating results which pertain to the AL II from those which may have occurred with the existing crane. There may not be adequate information available regarding the past performance of the existing crane, upon which to

base a comparison. If this *is* a difficulty, post audit will be less useful.

Changes to procedures

Proposed changes could incorporate any of the issues identified above (and more!). Some major points are listed below.

- Communication channels and consultation need to be improved.
- The financial analysis should focus on the NPV of investment opportunities, and the emphasis on PP should be minimal.
- Risk assessment and sensitivity analysis are crucial when assessing uncertain investments such as the AL II purchase, and do not seem to be adequately provided for, at present.
- The classifications of investments and their corresponding information requirements do not seem adequate and should be improved.
- The relationship between the January CI budget and the subsequent project approval procedures requires clarification. Budget-setting should be based on available financing and potential investment opportunities, rather than on some *ad hoc* adjustment to the previous year's budget.
- Required rate of return criteria appear to need review, and the CI manual should be specific about the use of real or nominal RRRs and cashflows.

SUMMARY

If CI decisions in the real world were as simple as the case presented here, there would be a lot of happy business people! In practice, there are often many more uncertainties, constraints and unforeseen outcomes.

However, this case has introduced the reader to some of the complexities of financially analysing CI proposals, and making decisions within an organizational context. There are no "correct" answers to this case. Readers may produce differing financial analyses, and may place greater or lesser weighting on the qualitative factors which might influence this CI decision. "Sophisticated" financial analyses go some way towards assisting CI decisions, but cannot alone provide the answers. Decision-makers must appreciate the value of these financial tools together with strategic considerations, market awareness and a sensitivity to organizational personnel.

It is important to be aware of the kinds of simplifying assumptions, estimates and judgements which form part of the complex practice of CI decision-making. People are important too, and this case has illustrated how personal attitudes, commitments and goals can complicate what we often like to see as a "rational" and objective decision process.

9

Conclusions

Before concluding by considering the future of capital investment decision-making theory and practice, it is useful to reflect on the ideas that have been presented so far.

REVIEW

At the outset, the reader was introduced to the nature and purpose of CI decision-making. It was noted that capital investment is an important determinant of the future success of many organizations. However, it is not an easy task. CI decision-making usually involves substantial financial outlay in return for future, uncertain returns. Poor CI decisions cannot only misdirect financial resources, but can undermine the future strategic direction and operations of the organization.

A model of the "CI decision-making process" was then introduced as a framework for discussing the various inputs to CI decisions. The traditional notion of CI decisions is that they occur as an ordered process, moving from the generation of investment ideas through to definition and screening, financial analysis, implementation and finally post audit. All of this takes place within an organizational environment, of which strategic planning and organizational personnel are two important aspects.

The reader was then introduced to techniques for the financial analysis of CI proposals. It was noted that those techniques which derive from economics theories of wealth maximization and risk aversion are considered most "sophisticated". Those techniques based on notions of accounting returns and liquidity, while often used in practice, are recognized as having fundamental flaws which reduce their usefulness for making rational economic decisions about CI projects. The increasing adoption of operations research techniques for decision support was noted, and tools for supporting risk analysis were outlined.

As the recommended technique for the financial analysis of CI proposals, NPV was explored in more detail in Chapter 4. Some practical issues of using NPV were considered, such as taxation effects, inflation, capital rationing and the comparison of projects with unequal lives. It was noted that, while NPV is the preferred analysis technique, it has some practical difficulties, as do all techniques in CI decision-making!

Some of the practical difficulties of the NPV method stem from the basic model's inability to take account of financial objectives other than maximization of the present value of cashflows. For example, most organizations operate under year–to–year liquidity constraints. Also, the importance of the financial reporting function cannot be ignored. Organizations are accountable to their stakeholders for performance, which is measured in accordance with accounting conventions and criteria such as profitability, rather than by considering discounted cashflows. Organizations must remain aware of the signals which their financial reports send to those stakeholders. For this reason, most organizations will be concerned with the effect of CI projects on their reported profitability and financial position. The NPV model alone does not take account of this.

"Pure" economic decision–making theory would dictate that liquidity constraints should not exist, as cash is always available where a project's returns can compensate for the cost of raising that cash (i.e. where NPV is positive). Similarly, accounting measures are seen as constructs which do not matter to the economic viability of a CI project. But theory aside, liquidity and reported profitability are real issues for most organizations. An NPV maximization model which can reflect these concerns therefore offers a practical alternative to the basic NPV approach. One way in which this could be achieved is by LP formulation, where relevant cashflows are input to the model, and total NPV is maximized subject to liquidity and profitability constraints in each time period.

However, using any form of NPV analysis still has some practical difficulties. The decision–maker must have some sense of a required rate of return (RRR) which CI projects must attain in order to be financially acceptable by NPV criteria. Approaches to determining this RRR were discussed in Chapter 5. The weighted average cost of capital (WACC) approach, in particular, was compared and contrasted with the market-orientated risk-adjusted CAPM approach. While the WACC approach has theoretical deficiencies, the sophisticated CAPM approach often has equally problematic practical difficulties. As a practical, but theoretically supported compromise, an "adjusted WACC" approach to determining the RRR was put forward. The main issue here was to obtain RRR measures which compensated for financing and opportunity costs, while taking into account the characteristic riskiness of a CI project.

Since the determination and treatment of risk is problematic, alternative approaches to assessing risky CIs were introduced. Such approaches included the use of probability distributions, simulation, sensitivity analysis and game theory. The utility of these approaches depends on the significance of risk in the project being assessed, and the information available to the decision-maker. Although in practice there is often insufficient information to allow a comprehensive application of these techniques, an awareness of risk effects is essential to CI decision-makers. Such decision support tools provide a framework for generating that awareness, and as such have great value in informing the CI decision.

Having considered theoretical approaches to analysing CI proposals, it was then appropriate to consider evidence for what happens in practice. Each element of the CI decision-making model was examined from an empirical perspective in Chapter 6. Overall, research evidence appears to suggest that there exists a "theory–practice gap" in the field of CI decision-making. Theoretically recommended techniques are not always used in practice, for no apparent good reason. There is also a clear dearth of empirical information relating to qualitative aspects of CI, particularly strategic planning, the stimulation and generation of investment ideas, and the role(s) of organizational personnel. The research evidence for CI practice has led academics to ponder possibilities of education time-lags, lack of resources, or sheer "irrationality" on the part of practitioners.

However, it is suggested in this text that there may be other reasons why observed practice does not match prescribed theory. Since theoretical developments in CI analysis have been grounded in theories of economic rationality, expectations of economically rational decision-making behaviour have ensued. However, the sociological literature tells us that it is reasonable to expect people to pursue alternative "rationalities". So, organizational, social and political forces may be just as strong as economic objectives in day-to-day CI decision-making. This has not been adequately recognized in CI theory development, nor in the exploration of practice, and may go some way towards explaining the apparent gap between theory and practice.

A broader view of CI decision-making within a social, political, organizational context has implications for the use of information provided by financial analyses. There are multiple potential uses for such financial information. The decision-maker must recognize the use(s) for which the information is required, and recognize also the contribution of this information as part (only) of a complex human decision-making process. Also, the importance of appropriate performance evaluation systems becomes apparent, when we consider the difficulties of motivating CI decision-makers to make "economically rational" choices.

This behavioural (and perhaps more complicated) view of CI decision-making is not designed to confuse, or to detract from the usefulness of appropriate financial analyses. Its function is rather to provide a balanced view. The reader, if he or she hopes to contribute usefully to CI decision-making practice, must be aware of the multidimensional nature of this activity. To illustrate (albeit simply) the issues of CI decision-making practice, a case and discussion were provided to prompt an appreciation of the complexity of "real" CI decisions.

So, here we are. By now the reader should feel comfortable with using (and interpreting the output of) recommended tools for the financial analysis of CI projects. Also it should be clear that, for successful CI decision-making, the organizational environment and personnel must support this important, strategic activity. Research evidence suggests that there are many ways in which practice can be improved to assist effective CI decision-making. Let us finish by considering some possible ways forward in developing the theory and practice of CI decision-making.

WHAT DOES THE FUTURE HOLD FOR CI DECISION-MAKING?

Determinants of the future of CI decision-making are twofold. The technical must balance with the organizational and social, and the CI activity must develop as part of a broader organizational context. Let us consider the two faces of the future of CI decision-making:

1. developments in CI analysis techniques
2. improvements in the CI decision-making environment.

Developments in CI analysis techniques

The "sophisticated" decision support tools developed for CI applications are constantly being revised and refined. Rigorous re-examination of the theoretical applicability of DCF approaches, together with greater attention to the demands of the real-world decision-making environment, provide the ongoing impetus for new perspectives on CI analysis. Also, the quantitative, mathematical capabilities of OR decision support techniques are being increasingly fine-tuned to CI analysis applications.

Some examples of advancements in CI decision-making models can be seen in discussions about finding appropriate costs of capital (or required rates of return) to use in conjunction with DCF analysis. Over many years authors have suggested ways of obtaining more accurate measures of the cost of capital. Usually this involves re-examination of the mathematical models used to compute factors such as the cost of debt and equity capital, and/or alternative approaches to incorporating risk into the RRR. Recent examples of such work include considerations of better estimating the cost of equity capital (Ben-Horim and Callen, 1989), and assessing the systematic risk of industry segments, for use with CAPM approaches (Crum and Bi, 1988).

All of these research works contribute to our growing appreci-ation of how mathematical and economic models can be more accurately (and, we hope, practically) applied to CI decision-making.

Other areas of theoretical development include the treatment of inflation and improved use of forecasting techniques to assist in obtaining the required information for assessing future cashflows. Along these lines, general areas of management accounting and finance interest, such as information economics, offer increasing contributions to CI decision-making. With more and more sophisticated techniques offering improved ways of manipulating financial information, the question increasingly becomes: when is it worth gathering even more information? Information economics offers mechanisms for assessing the cost–benefit balance in obtaining decision-making information, and has practical impli-cations for CI decision-making under conditions of limited time and monetary resources.

The contribution of OR techniques to CI decision-making continues to receive attention in theoretical literature. OR-type models are refined and adapted to allow improved application to real-world CI decisions. For example, recent work has considered improvements to the application of sensitivity analysis (Darvish and Eckstein, 1988), multi-criteria decision-making (Venugopal and Narendran, 1990), and the use of mathematical models in considering uncertainty (Levary, 1988; Kira and Kusy, 1990).

Pike and Sharp (1989) have noted the strong increase in the uptake of OR techniques from 1975 to 1986. They also propose that, while the rate of increase is likely to slow, the use of almost all OR techniques in CI decision-making is set to continue increasing. So, it seems that advances in theoretical applications of OR methods to CI are increasingly informing practice, and it appears likely that continued developments in these "sophisticated" methods will have a significant impact on future CI decision-making.

It is beyond the scope of this book to examine the detail of these more complex presentations of the decision support tools introduced earlier. However, it is significant that refinement of such techniques is one way in which the outputs of financial CI analyses can be made more accurate and useful. However, such theoretical refinements do not always solve the problems of practice, where information, time and understanding of complex mathematics may be in short supply. Let us now consider the other face of improving CI practice – people.

Improving the CI decision-making environment

Effective CI decision-making relies as much on the organizational environment and people as it does on sophisticated analysis techniques. There are several ways in which the organizational environment and functions can support the CI decision-making activity. Below, we shall consider the potential for development in some of these areas.

Encouraging and capitalizing on CI project ideas

No matter how elaborate and sophisticated an organization's attention to CI is, little can be accomplished without good CI ideas. This is especially true as we move further into an age where innovation is crucial to the success of many organizations. It has already been noted that the stimulation and generation of CI ideas is one of the more neglected stages of the CI process, and little is known of how ideas are generated in practice.

Organizational personnel may often feel reluctant to present their ideas for discussion and development in the CI arena. The risk of trying and failing may be perceived as greater than the potential reward from hitting upon a successful CI suggestion. Also, there are not always adequate communication channels which permit ideas to emerge from all levels of the organization.

It has been suggested that many CI ideas come from people occupying relatively low positions in the organizational hierarchy (Mukherjee and Henderson, 1987). It is often these people who have hands-on experience at the operating level, and who can envisage potential for improvement in current practices. If they are not encouraged to come forward with their ideas, or those ideas are not communicated to the appropriate people, the organization is the poorer for it.

Hertenstein (1990) has suggested ways in which organizational personnel can be encouraged to contribute to CI idea-generation. She suggests that it is important to recognize non-financial information as being equally important to financial information. This will encourage project proposers to develop projects which provide strategic benefits, even if the proposers lack the skill or data necessary to express the projects in financial terms.

Also, Hertenstein suggests that some people may be reluctant to put forward ideas where they do not feel confident with all aspects of the project. Subjecting project proposals to interfunc-tional, interdisciplinary review can help to overcome this problem. The knowledge that a proposal will be reviewed by people with appropriate expertise relieves the proposer of the responsibility of knowing all potential aspects of the project. People are then free to suggest ideas which they consider to have potential merit, even if they cannot fully capture all its strategic or financial implications.

Finally, Hertenstein suggests that early review of CI proposals can encourage broad, comprehensive evaluation of all types of projects. The use of effective pre-screening programmes allows valuable opportunities to be recognized *before* any difficult financial analysis is required. Project proposers are therefore encouraged to come forward with CI ideas, knowing that they will not be wasting large amounts of organizational time and resources if their ideas turn out to be unfruitful. Similarly, inappropriate CI ideas can be eliminated before the proposer has had any need to accumulate wider commitment to the project, thus risking public humiliation if the idea is not pursued.

It is important to the promotion of effective CI decision-making that CI ideas be encouraged from organizational personnel. Attention to the organizational environment is vital. Attitudes to CI suggestions, pre-screening procedures and performance appraisal and reward systems are all-important factors in gaining the most benefit from the collective expertise and innovation of organizational personnel.

Integrating CI with strategic planning and decision-making

It has already been noted that CI can be viewed as an integral part of strategic planning and decision-making. The long-term objectives of an organization can only be met if long-term investments in productive capital, technology and marketing are directed towards these objectives. Increasingly, CI decisions are referred to as "strategic investments", reflecting a growing awareness of this link between investment and strategy.

Barwise, Marsh and Wensley (1989) note the importance of strategic factors (such as marketing) to good CI decision-making. They suggest (p. 85) that two marketing issues are central to a successful CI project:

- The product or service concerned must have "enough value to enough customers to support prices and volumes that exceed the costs of supplying it – including the opportunity cost of capital".
- The organization must have "enough sources of sustainable competitive advantage to exploit, develop and defend the opportunity".

Barwise, Marsh and Wensley (p. 85) note that "good analysis ties the details of strategy to the financial implications". They point out the need to treat financial analysis of CI projects as part of a broader strategic analysis, lamenting (p. 90) that ". . . the financial analysis is all too often 'pinned on' afterward, rather like the tail on the donkey in the children's game".

An integrated, interactive approach to CI decision-making as part of the strategic planning activity adds depth and direction to investment decisions. While financial analyses have an important part to play, they cannot produce meaningful answers without a consideration of the organization's strategic objectives and environment. Increasing recognition of this link between strategy and CI presents a significant opportunity for advancement in effective CI decision-making.

Improving post audit

The post audit feedback phase of the CI activity appears to be one of the most neglected areas of CI practice. Of course, conducting post audits can be costly in terms of time and information resources, and so many organizations post audit only selected projects. However, much of the potential benefit of conducting post audits is lost where appropriate information is lacking, or where the results are not appropriately incorporated into future considerations of CI decision-making.

Neale and Holmes (1990) make several observations about ways in which post audit can be effectively implemented.[1] An important issue is acceptance of the post audit system by organizational personnel. Neale and Holmes (p. 92) noted that the system must be "skilfully presented, perhaps as an expression of interest rather than as an inquisition into particular activities". If this is achieved, organizational personnel are more likely to feel positive about an opportunity to display their competence, rather than feeling negative about being "checked up on".

Also, good post audit requires that information systems are able to provide appropriate details of projects' performance. Neale and Holmes (p. 93) refer to a "disentanglement problem", that is, a difficulty in identifying the specific results of a single project, as distinct from all other organizational activities. They also observe (p. 93) that post audit of existing projects may be more trouble than it is worth. It may be better to "announce the PA [post audit] of new projects and to carefully specify beforehand the expected costs and benefits from the project in a form compatible with their subsequent investigation".

Financial reporting and information systems must be designed so as to facilitate the collection of data suitable for comparison with initial project approvals. This can be a costly exercise if significant redesigning of existing systems is required. However, there is little to be gained from using an accrual-based accounting system to provide feedback on projects which are incremental in nature and cashflow-based.

Strategic factors again arise as an important aspect of effective PA. Neale and Holmes (p. 93) refer to the need for post audit to be balanced between numerical analysis and consideration of strategic factors. They note practitioners' attitudes to this balance: "excessive concern with numerical data may deter staff at the divisional level – ('yet more data to collect') and damage their enthusiasm and co-operation for the whole procedure". On the other hand, there is a danger that "strategic considerations may be used as a smoke-screen to hide below-par performance".

---

[1] Neale and Holmes based their conclusions on an extensive 1985 survey of 384 firms, from which they compared the responses of users and non-users of post audit procedures.

Clearly, the balance between financial and strategic performance must be clearly specified so that commitment is retained while still assuring tangible accountability. Finally, the way in which post audit information is fed back into the CI decision-making activity is important. Neale and Holmes (p. 94) note that post audit information, together with board (of directors) comments should be "fed back to the original project analysts to indicate the areas in which it was felt that the initial evaluation had been deficient. Project analysts should be given the opportunity to discuss the results of the PA in a constructive fashion rather than the exercise be seen as a 'finger-pointing exercise'."

The incorporation of these issues into the design and use of PA systems provides a means for improving CI decision-making which has yet to be capitalized on by many organizations. Strengthening the "feedback loop" of the decision activity will provide for increased learning, and ongoing improvements in CI decision-making. This is clearly an area for future development.

Increasing levels of education about CI techniques and approaches

This is where you come into the picture! As more people who have knowledge of CI techniques and approaches enter organizations, the level of technical competence in CI decision-making will rise. Although much of the basic CI theory has been around for over thirty years, many CI decision-makers have not had the opportunity to learn the correct application of these techniques. Increased education will continue to help close the gap between CI theory and practice.

However, balance is important as well. No amount of technically skilled, numerate management accounting and finance graduates will improve CI decision-making practice unless they appreciate the organizational context of the CI activity. Yet, increased numbers of educated practitioners, greater awareness of the "sophisticated" decision support tools offered by economics and OR models, and widespread availability of computers is certain to impact on the future of CI decision-making. Whether or not that impact is constructive is a much more complex issue, requiring an informed, balanced perspective on the part of CI decision-makers.

Idea generation, the strategic focus, post audit and education are just four issues which will contribute to the shaping of CI decision-making in the future. There are, without doubt, other equally important factors, some which may not even have been imagined yet! Capital investment practice has seen many changes over the last three decades, and will no doubt see many more in the years ahead. What those changes are remains to be seen.

CONCLUSION: THE INFORMATION-PROVIDER AND CI DECISION-MAKING

Once the sophisticated financial analyses provided by CI decision support techniques are performed, it becomes the task of the information-provider to communicate this information to the CI decision-makers. This communication will be ineffective if:

1. the message is incorrect (i.e. the financial results are not correctly calculated)
2. appropriate communication channels are not available
3. the "receiver" is not prepared to hear the message.

In addition, the "receiver", or CI decision-maker, must be able to interpret and act on the financial information in a way which takes account of broader strategic issues, and meets the decision objectives (whether these be economic, social, or political).

The combination of technical competence and a supportive decision environment is crucial to the ongoing success and future development of CI decision-making within any organization. The job of the information-provider (often the accountant or financial controller) is to provide the technical competence, while being cognisant of the ways in which this information will be used so that appropriate formats for its presentation can be developed.

Perhaps one of the most important benefits of technical competence is knowing what to look for. Rather than furnishing "the answer", sophisticated CI decision support techniques provide a framework for those people who are *looking for* "the answer". The investigative rigour imposed by financial analysis forces decision-makers to consider the market, cashflows, physical logistics, financing requirements, and other key variables of any CI project. Without the need to provide financial justification for CI projects, many of these factors may be overlooked.

In the overall scheme of the CI decision-making activity, the information-provider is both master and servant. Servant, because he or she must provide information which is useful to those people who are charged with making the CI decision. Master, because the information presented, and the way in which it is presented, can significantly shape the final decision. In the end, it is people who will take action based on the numbers. Both people and process are important, as both determine success or failure in the CI decision-making activity.

References

Aharoni, Y. (1966). *The Foreign Investment Decision Proccess*, Division of Research, Harvard Business School.

Alfred, A.M. (1964). *Discounted Cash Flow and Corporate Planning*. Lecture delivered to the Woolwich Polytechnic, UK, 8 May, as part of a Symposium on Economic Planning, *Woolwich Economic Papers*, No. 5.

Allison, G.T. (1969). "Conceptual models and the Cuban missile crisis", *The American Political Science Review*, Vol. 63 (3), September, pp. 689–718.

Bailes, J.C. and McNally, G.M. (1984). "Cost and management accounting practices in New Zealand", *International Journal of Accounting Education and Research*, Vol. 19 (Spring), pp. 59–71.

Baker, J.C. (1981). "Capital budgeting in West European companies", *Management Decision*, Vol. 19 (1), pp. 3–11.

Barwise, P., Marsh, P.R. and Wensley, R. (1989). "Must finance and strategy clash?", *Harvard Business Review*, September–October, pp. 85–90.

Bavishi, V.B. (1981). "Capital budgeting practice at multinationals", *Management Accounting (US)*, August, pp. 32–5.

Baxter, J.A. and Hirst, M.K. (1986). *A capital budgeting case study: an analysis of a choice process and the role of information*, University of New South Wales, Department of Accounting Working Paper Series No. 58, January.

Ben-Horim, M. and Callen, J.L. (1989). "The cost of capital, Macaulay's duration, and Tobin's q", *Journal of Financial Research*, Vol. 12 (2), Summer, pp. 143–56.

Berg, N.A. (1965). "Strategic planning in conglomerate companies", *Harvard Business Review*, November–December, pp. 32–40.

Bower, J.L. (1970). *Managing the Resource Allocation Process: A Study of Corporate Planning and Investment*, Richard D. Irwin Inc.: Homewood, Illinois.

Brealey, R.A. and Myers, S.C. (1984). *Principles of Corporate Finance*, International Student Edition, McGraw-Hill Inc.: New York.

Brealey, R.A. and Myers, S.C. (1991). *Principles of Corporate Finance* (4th edn.), McGraw-Hill Inc.: New York.

Brigham, E.F. (1975). "Hurdle rates for screening capital expenditure proposals", *Financial Management*, Vol. 4 (3), Autumn, pp. 17–26.

Burchell, S., Clubb, C., Hopwood, A., Hughes, J. and Nahapiet, J. (1980). "The roles of accounting in organizations and society", *Accounting, Organizations and Society*, Vol. 5 (1), pp. 5–27.

Butler, R., Davies, L., Pike, R. and Sharp, J. (1991). "Strategic investment decision-making: Complexities, politics and processes", *Journal of Management Studies*, Vol. 28 (4), July, pp. 395–415.

Christy, G.A. (1966). *Capital Budgeting – Current Practices and their Efficiency*. Eugene: Bureau of Business and Economic Research, University of Oregon.

Chua, W.F. (1988). "Accounting as a social practice in organisations: A critical review", Proceedings of the Management Accounting Research Conference, University of New South Wales, September.

Churchman, C.W. (1968). *Challenge to Reason*, McGraw-Hill: New York.

Cooper, D.J. (1975). "Rationality and investment appraisal", *Accounting and Business Research*, No. 19, Summer, pp. 198–202.

Crum, R.L. and Bi, K. (1988). "An observation on estimating the systematic risk of an industry segment", *Financial Management*, Vol. 17 (1), Spring, pp. 60–2.

Darvish, T. and Eckstein, S. (1988). "A model for simultaneous sensitivity analysis of projects", *Applied Economics (UK)*, Vol. 20 (1), January, pp. 113–23.

Emmanuel, C., Otley, D. and Merchant, K. (1990). *Accounting for Management Control* (2nd edn.), Chapman and Hall: London.

Fremgen, J.M. (1973). "Capital budgeting practices: a survey", *Management Accounting (US)*, May, pp. 19–25.

Gimpl, M.L. and Dakin, S.R. (1984). "Management and magic", *California Management Review*, Vol. 27 (1), Fall, pp. 125–36.

Gitman, L.J. and Forrester, J.R. (1977). "A survey of capital budgeting techniques used by major U.S. firms", *Financial Management*, Fall, pp. 66–71.

Haka, S.F. (1987). "Capital budgeting techniques and firm specific contingencies: A correlational analysis", *Accounting, Organizations and Society*, Vol. 12 (1), pp. 31–48.

Haka, S.F., Gordon, L.A. and Pinches, G.E. (1985). "Sophisticated capital budgeted techniques and firm performance", *The Accounting Review*, Vol. 60 (4), October, pp. 651–69.

Hastie, K.L. (1974). "One businessman's view of capital budgeting", *Financial Management* (Winter), pp. 36–44.

Hendricks, J.A. (1981). "Capital budgeting practices including inflation adjustments: a survey", *Managerial Planning*, January/February, pp. 22–8.

Hertenstein, J.H. (1990). "Behavior in capital budgeting: Capital budgeting procedures and the process of initiating capital investment proposals", paper presented at the American Accounting Association Conference, Toronto, August.

Hertz, D.B. (1964). "Risk analysis in capital investment", *Harvard Business Review*, January–February, pp. 175–86.

Ho, S.S.M. and Pike, R.H. (1991). "Risk analysis in capital budgeting contexts: Simple or sophisticated?, *Accounting and Business Research*, Vol. 21 (83), pp. 227–38.

Hogarth, R.M. and Makridakis, S. (1981). "Forecasting and planning: An evaluation", *Management Science*, Vol. 27 (2), pp. 115–38.

Hollis, M. and Nell, E.J. (1975). *Rational Economic Man: A Philosophical Critique of Neo-Classical Economics*, Cambridge University Press: London.

Horngren, C.T. and Foster, G. (1987). *Cost Accounting: A Managerial Emphasis* (6th edn.), Prentice-Hall Inc.: Englewood Cliffs, N.J.

Horngren, C.T. and Foster, G. (1991). *Cost Accounting: A Managerial Emphasis* (7th edn.), Prentice-Hall Inc.: Englewood Cliffs, N.J.

Hosseini, H. (1990). "The archaic, the obsolete and the mythical in neoclassical economic problems with the rationality and optimizing assumptions of the Jevons–Marshallian system", *American Journal of Economics and Sociology*, Vol. 49 (1), January, pp. 81–92.

Istvan, D.F. (1961a). "The economic evaluation of capital expenditures", *Journal of Business*, Vol. 34, January, p. 45.

Istvan, D.F. (1961b). *Capital Expenditure Decisions: How they are Made in Large Corporations*, Bureau of Business Research, Indiana University: Bloomington.

Jones, C. (1989). "Understanding Management Accountants: The Rationality of Social Action" (unpublished), Department of Economics and Social Science, Bristol Polytechnic.

Kelly, M. and Pratt, M.J. (1989). "Management accounting: Perceived purpose and choice of approach", Proceedings of the Accounting Association of Australia and New Zealand Annual Conference (Vol. 2), July, Melbourne, Australia.

Keown, A.J., Scott, D.F., Martin, J.D. and Petty, J.W. (1985). *Basic Financial Management* (3rd edn.), Prentice-Hall Inc.: Englewood Cliffs, N.J.

Kim, S.H. (1982). "An empirical study on the relationship between capital budgeting practices and earnings performance", *Engineering Economist*, Vol. 27 (3), pp. 185–96.

Kim, S.H. and Farragher, E.J. (1981). "Current capital budgeting practices", *Management Accounting (US)*, June, pp. 26–30.

King, P. (1975). "Is the emphasis of capital budgeting theory misplaced?", *Journal of Business Finance and Accounting*, Vol. 2 (1), pp. 69–82.

Kira, D.S. and Kusy, M.I. (1990). "A stochastic capital rationing model", *Journal of the Operational Research Society (UK)*, Vol. 41 (9), September, pp. 853–63.

Klammer, T.P. (1972). "Empirical evidence of the adoption of sophisticated capital budgeting techniques", *The Journal of Business*, July, pp. 387–97.

Klammer, T.P. (1973). "The association of capital budgeting techniques with firm performance", *The Accounting Review*, Vol. 48 (2), April, pp. 353–64.

Klammer, T.P. and Walker, M.C. (1984). "The continuing increase in the use of sophisticated capital budgeting techniques", *California Management Review*, pp. 135–48.

Lapsley, I. (1986). "Investment appraisal in public service organisations", *Management Accounting (UK)*, Vol. 64 (3), pp. 28–31.

Levary, R.R. (1988). "A sequential solution procedure to stochastic capital budgeting models", *Computers and Industrial Engineering*, Vol. 14 (4), pp. 371–80.

Levy, H. and Sarnat, M. (1978). *Capital Investment and Financial Decisions*, Prentice-Hall International.

Levy, H. and Sarnat, M. (1982). *Capital Investment and Financial Decisions* (2nd edn.), Prentice-Hall International.

Lilleyman, P.G. (1984). "Capital budgeting: current practices of Australian organizations", *The Australian Accountant*, Vol. 54 (2), March, pp. 130–3.

Lindblom, C.E. (1968). *The Policy-Making Process*, Prentice-Hall: New York.

Mao, J.C.T. (1970). "Survey of capital budgeting: theory and practice", *The Journal of Finance*, Vol. 25 (2), May, pp. 349–60.

March, J.G. and Olsen, J.P. (1976). *Ambiguity and Choice in Organizations*, Universitetsforlaget: Bergen.

Marsh, P., Barwise, P., Thomas, K. and Wensley, R. (1988). *Managing Strategic Investment Decisions in Large Diversified Companies*, London Business School: London.

McIntyre, A. and Coulthurst, N. (1987). "Planning and control of capital investment in medium-sized UK companies", *Management Accounting (UK)*, March, pp. 39–40.

McMahon, R.G.P. (1981). "The determination and use of investment hurdle rates in capital budgeting: A survey of Australian practice", *Accounting and Finance*, Vol. 21 (1), May, pp. 15–25.

McNally, G.M. (1980). *Cost and Management Accounting in New Zealand: A Survey of the Practices Used in Manufacturing Companies*, Cost and Management Accounting Division, New Zealand Society of Accountants: Wellington.

Meredith, G.G. (1964). "Administrative control of capital expenditures: A survey of Australian public companies", *University of Queensland Papers*, Vol. 1 (2), September, pp. 35–52.

Meredith, G.G. (1965). "Capital rationing and the determination of the firm's performance standards for capital investment analysis", *University of Queensland Papers*, Vol. 1 (4), December, pp. 85–114.

Merrett, A.J. and Sykes, A. (1963). *The Finance and Analysis of Capital Projects*, Longmans Green & Co. Ltd: London.

Miller, P. (1988). "Managing Economic Growth Through Knowledge: The Invention, Promotion and Deployment of Discounted Cash Flow Techniques" (unpublished), London School of Economics and Political Science: London.

Mills, R.W. (1988). "Capital budgeting techniques used in the UK and the USA", *Management Accounting (UK)*, Vol. 66 (1), January, pp. 26–7.

Mintzberg, H., Raisinghani, D. and Theoret, A. (1976). "The structure of 'unstructured' decision processes", *Administrative Science Quarterly*, Vol. 21, June, pp. 246–75.

Moore, J.S. and Reichert, A.K. (1983). "An analysis of the financial management techniques currently employed by large US corporations", *Journal of Business Finance and Accounting*, Vol. 10 (4), pp. 623–45.

Mukherjee, T.K. and Henderson, G.V. (1987). "The capital budgeting process: Theory and practice", *Interfaces*, Vol. 17 (2), March–April, pp. 78–90.

Neale, C.W. and Holmes, D.E.A. (1990). "Post-Auditing capital projects", *Long Range Planning*, Vol. 23 (4), pp. 88–96.

Northcott, D.N. (1991). "Rationality and decision making in capital budgeting", *British Acccounting Review*, Vol. 23 (3), September, pp. 219–34.

Oblak, D.J. and Helm, R.J. (1980). "Survey and analysis of capital budgeting methods used by multinationals", *Financial Management*, Vol. 9, Winter, pp. 37–41.

Patterson, C.S. (1989). "Investment decision criteria used by listed New Zealand companies", *Accounting and Finance*, Vol. 29 (2), November, pp. 73–89.

Perera, P. (1988–9). "Capital budgeting by MICs", *Professional Administrator*, Vol. 40 (6), November–January, pp. 22–4.

Petry, G.H. (1975). "Effective use of capital budgeting tools", *Business Horizons*, October, pp. 57–65.

Petty, J.W. and Scott, D.F. (1981). "Capital budgeting practices in large U.S. firms: A retrospective analysis and update". In Derkinderen, I. and Crum, R.L. (eds), *Readings in Strategy for Corporate Investment*, Pitman, Boston, pp. 9–30.

Petty, J.W., Scott, D.F. and Bird, M.M. (1975). "The capital expenditure decision-making process of large corporations", *The Engineering Economist*, Vol. 20 (3), Spring, pp. 159–71.

Pike, R.H. (1982). *Capital Budgeting in the 1980s: A Major Survey of the Investment Practices in Large Companies*. CIMA.

Pike, R.H. (1983a). "The capital budgeting behaviour and corporate characteristics of capital-constrained firms", *Journal of Business Finance and Accounting*, Vol. 10 (4), Winter, pp. 663–71.

Pike, R.H. (1983b). "A review of recent trends in formal capital budgeting processes", *Accounting and Business Research*, Vol. 51, Summer, pp. 201–8.

Pike, R.H. (1984). "DCF trends and the problem of nonresponse bias", *Managerial Finance*, Vol. 10 (3/4), pp. 49–52.

Pike, R.H. (1988). "An empirical study of the adoption of sophisticated capital budgeting practices and decision-making effectiveness", *Accounting and Business Research*, Vol. 18 (72), pp. 341–51.

Pike, R.H. and Dobbins, R. (1986). *Investment Decisions and Financial Strategy*, Philip Allan Ltd: Oxford.

Pike, R.H. and Sharp, J. (1989). "Trends in the use of management science techniques in capital budgeting", *Managerial and Decision Economics*, Vol. 10, pp. 135–40.

Pike, R.H. and Wolfe, M.B. (1988). *Capital Budgeting for the 1990s: A Review of Capital Investment Trends in Larger Companies*, The Chartered Institute of Management Accountants (Occasional Paper Series), London.

Pullara, S.J. and Walker, L.R. (1965). "The evaluation of capital expenditure proposals: A survey of firms in the chemical industry", *The Journal of Business*, Vol. 38 (4), October, pp. 403–8.

Rappaport, A. (1979). "A critique of capital budgeting questionnaires", *Interfaces*, Vol. 9 (3), May, pp. 100–5.

Rosenblatt, M.J. and Jucker, J.V. (1979). "Capital expenditure decision-making: Some tools and trends", *Interfaces*, Vol. 9 (2), Pt. 1, February, pp. 63–9.

Ross, M. (1986). "Capital budgeting practices of twelve large manufacturers", *Financial Management*, Vol. 15 (4), Winter, pp. 15–22.

Runyon, L.R. (1983). "Capital expenditure decision making in small firms", *Journal of Business Research*, Vol. 11 (3), September, pp. 389–97.

Scapens, R.W. and Sale, J.T. (1981). "Performance measurement and formal capital expenditure controls in divisionalised companies", *Journal of Business Finance and Accounting*, Vol. 8 (3), pp. 389–419.

Schall, L.D., Sundem, G.L. and Geijsbeek, W.R. (1978). "Survey and analysis of capital budgeting methods", *The Journal of Finance*, Vol. 33 (1), March, pp. 281–6.

Scott, D.F., Gray, O.P. and Bird, M.M. (1972). "Investing and financing behavior of small manufacturing firms", *MSU Business Topics*, Vol. 20, Summer, pp. 29–38.

Singer, A.E. (1985). "Strategic and financial decision-making processes in New Zealand public companies", *New Zealand Journal of Business*, Vol. 7, pp. 33–46.

Soldofsky, R.M. (1971). "The what, why, and how of capital budgeting for smaller businesses". In Serraino, W.J., Singhvi, S.S. and Soldofsky, R.M., *Frontiers of Financial Management*, South-Western Publishing Co.: Ohio, USA, pp. 21–38.

Stanley, M.T. and Block, S.B. (1984). "A survey of multinational capital budgeting", *The Financial Review*, pp. 36–54.

Venugopal, V. and Narendran, T.T. (1990). "An interactive procedure for multiobjective optimization using Nash bargaining principles", *Decision Support Ssytems*, Vol. 6 (3), August, pp. 261–8.

Weber, M. (1961). *General Economic Theory*, Collier Books: New York.

Wilson, R.M.S. and Chua, W.F. (1988). *Managerial Accounting: Method and Meaning*, Van Nostrand Reinhold (International) Co. Ltd: London.

APPENDIX: EXAMPLES OF STANDARD FORMS FOR A CAPITAL INVESTMENT PROPOSAL

(These forms are modelled on those used by a large organization.)

HYPOTHETICAL CORPORATION

CAPITAL INVESTMENT

DIVISION: _____   TOTAL AMOUNT REQUESTED: $ _____

LOCATION: _____   DEPARTMENT: _____

PROJECT NAME: _____   APPLICATION NO: _____

_____   DATE: _____

INDICATE CLASSIFICATION:

☐ NEW BUSINESS   ☐ SAFETY/ENVIRONMENT

☐ EXISTING BUSINESS EXPANSION   ☐ QUALITY·

☐ COST REDUCTION   ☐ REPLACEMENT

EXPENDITURE SUMMARY		
Initial Outlay		
Future		
Expenditures		
= Requested Amounts		
Plus Related Expenses		
= Total Investment	$	
Amount Authorised	$	

FINANCIAL JUSTIFICATION

Year	0	1	2	3	4	5
Net Cashflow*						
Less Depn.						
Net Profit						
* Enter from Section 5						

SOURCE OF FUNDING
Budgeted ☐ (Tick)

Year	Category	IRR/NPV	Priority	$ Budgeted

Budgeted ☐ (Tick)

AVERAGE NET PROFITS/SAVINGS
OVER FIVE YEARS $ _____

PAYBACK (YEARS)   _____

NPV @ ____ % =   _____

IRR   =   _____

PROJECT LIFE   =   _____ Years

SUBMITTED BY:	Name	Signature	Date	APPROVED BY:	Signature	Date
Initiator				Division Manager		
Project Leader				General Manager		
Accountant				Group Eng. Manager		
Engineer						

CORPORATE APPROVALS	Name	Signature	Date			
Capex Controller						
Financial Controller				Group General Manager		
				Chief Executive		

1. PROJECT DESCRIPTION, OBJECTIVES AND RELEVANCE TO STRATEGY

2. DETAILS OF PRESENT PLANT/EQUIPMENT

Description of Present Plant	Age (Years)	BOOK VALUE $ Date	Est. Residual Value $

What is proposed to be done with present equipment?

3. SUMMARY OF SUPPLY QUOTATIONS OBTAINED

Project Component	Chosen Supplier	$	2nd Supplier	$	3rd Supplier	$

4. PROJECT COST BREAKDOWN Show the Project Cost Breakdown Below:	APPLICATION NO:					
YEAR	0	1	2	3	4	5
DIRECT PROJECT COST: Land and Buildings Plant & Equipment Installation Furniture/Office Equipment Consultants Fees Computer Hardware & Software Import Duty Freight and Insurance Building Permits/Local Body Levies Other						
Total Direct Project Cost						
RELATED EXPENSES: Feasibility Study & Evaluation Commissioning Costs Documentation and Manuals Staff Training/Recruitment/Redundancy Accounting Software Costs Other						
Total Related Expenses						

CONTINGENCIES AND WORKING CAPITAL
Currency (Forex) Provision
 	
General Contingency
 	
Net Working Capital - Inventories
          - Debtors
          - Spares
Other						

Total Contingencies Etc. **Less Residual Value of existing assets**						
= TOTAL INVESTMENT **$**						
Less Total Related Expenses Less Net Working Capital						
= Requested Amount **(Enter on front page)** **$**						

NOTE: - Total investment figure to be used to calculate project IRR, NPV, payback and return on original investment.
     - Related expenses are fully tax deductible and are to be expensed in Year 1 for accounting purposes.

5. INCOME AND EXPENDITURE CALCULATIONS (Complete only for IRR projects)

Show full calculations by way of attachment and summarise the costs and benefits below:

ANNUAL OPERATIVE ADVANTAGE FROM NEW ASSET	Increase Costs	Decrease Costs	Balance
	Decrease Revenue $	Increase Revenue $	$
REVENUE (Details on Separate Sheet)			
LESS COSTS			
Components			
Wages, Salaries and Allowances			
Packaging Materials			
Consumables/Other Materials			
Storage and Handling			
Freight			
Repairs and Maintenance			
Energy			
Cleaning			
Vehicle Expenses			
Insurance, Rents, Leases			
Administration, Selling Expenses			
Other			
Total Change of Costs/Expenses			
= Net Cash Flow			
		† Enter Page 1 of Capex	

NOTES:
- Where revenue and cost projections for years 2-5 will differ from year 1, show by attachment.
- Savings per the above able represent promised cash benefits.

Post Audit
Who will audit the project and when?

	APPLICATION NO.

6. ALTERNATIVES CONSIDERED AND REASON FOR REJECTION

What alternatives have been considered?

What are the consequences of not doing the project now?

What are the consequences of doing project only partially now?

7. TIMING AND MILESTONES

When is approval required by?

When will orders be placed?

When will the project be commissioned?

8. SENSITIVITY ANALYSIS

Identify below those critical project parameters (eg. changes in throughput) which will impact on the projects IRR should events turn out differently to planned.

Show in the table below the project IRR's assuming the expected, pessimistic and most pessimistic outcome of the critical parameters identified above.

Outcome	% Movement in Critical Parameter	Internal Rate of Return
Expected	_____	_____
Pessimistic	_____	_____
Most Pessimistic	_____	_____

Index